Free To LEAD

The Doctor's Guide to Profitable Leadership Performance

Betty Derricott

New Day Publishing
Tigard, Oregon

Free to Lead:

The Doctor's Guide to Profitable Leadership Performance

by Betty Derricott

Derricott Dental Management
6975 SW Sandburg, Suite 130-7
Tigard, Oregon 97223

Library of Congress Catalog Card Number: 93-74929

ISBN-0-9640156-0-9

Published by New Day Publishing
6975 SW Sandburg, Suite 130-7
Tigard, Oregon 97223

Cover design by Kim McLaughlin.
Illustrations by Kim McLaughlin and Martha Khoury.

Printed and bound in the United States of America.

First edition, first printing.

1 2 3 4 5 6 7 8 9 10

Dedicated to the healing process.

TABLE OF CONTENTS

MEET BETTY DERRICOTT

Betty Derricott speaks with the authority that can be gained only through experience. With a lifelong career centered in the dental office, she has felt the pain of conflict and the triumph of cooperation.

Committed to a healthy work environment and to the unlimited potential of growing human beings, she provides a unique bridge between doctors and their employees. This "Doctors Guide to Profitable Leadership Performance" provides step-by-step direction in the process of developing personal accountability and team synergy.

In this book and in her training presentations, Betty's mission is to challenge every person with the option to be *free to lead.*

Betty Derricott is a member of the Academy of Dental Management Consultants, the American Society for Training and Development, and the Consultants Executive Network. She is a frequent speaker and facilitator of group learning.

ACKNOWLEDGMENTS

This book is a testimony to the awesome power that is awakened through vision, purpose, and intention.

The experience of pushing past my personal limitations and fear allowed me to connect with an army of allies who were to join with me in the creation of this work.

It is miraculous how every resource and insight were there at precisely the right time. It validates my faith in the wisdom of creation and our human inter-connection.

My heart is full of gratitude for the abundance of support, encouragement, and inspiration that were provided.

To the people who brought together the resources and technical know-how, acknowledgments! You are the best of the best.

Ellen Campbell put together the publishing team. She provided the resources, answers, questions, and ideas. I acknowledge and thank you, Ellen, as a marketing consultant, context editor, and genuine friend.

Martha Khoury is the impeccable editor and format designer. She systematically organized my scattered ideas into words, sentences, and paragraphs. She always believed in my vision and, at the same time, kept me grounded in reality. I thank you, Martha, for your patience, confidence, and unfaltering attention to detail.

David Moline is a highly-regarded dentist and friend. With broad academic and professional experience, he volunteered to participate in leadership study groups for a year to review my work, and, eventually, to write the foreword for this book. David, your confidence and support have been an invaluable gift to me. Thank you.

Kim McLaughlin is an artist. She created the cover that makes the book. Her work speaks for itself. Thank you, Kim.

To my family:

- My father, Clifford J. Samson, who recently celebrated 90 years of life, thank you for your example of honesty, integrity, and common-sense respect for others. And in memory of my mother, Sophie Samson, I celebrate her spirit of perseverance and creative enterprise. Thank you.
- Ron, my husband, you are my friend, my coach, my teacher, and the love of my life. Thank you for all you are and for being in my life.
- Children and grandchildren, you are a joy in my life that makes me more complete.
- Debbie, my daughter, you bring me inspiration, joy, and insight. You are a genuine angel.
- Tim, my son, you are an artist of ideas, concepts, and music. Your songs inspire me. Your friendship is treasured.

And to all the other companions on my journey of becoming, I honor you: Eileen Hannegan, who challenged me to write; Marie Chavarria, my spiritual guide to courage; and Sheryl Burnham, my best friend, who nurtured the first ideas into a training manual.

To the dentists who employed me and provided me with opportunities to learn and contribute, I thank you.

To my many clients, committed to being the best dentists, business people, and leaders that they can be, I acknowledge you.

To the professionals who work as dental assistants, hygienists, technicians, and administrators, I salute you for your commitment to serve. You are a source of healing.

To my associates in the Academy of Dental Management Consultants, who are committed to the integrity of our profession and to the contribution we bring to dentistry, I thank you. To the women of the Consultants Executive Network, who brought me courage to complete this project, thank you.

Especially to the many dentists who participated in the process of Authentic Leadership Certification and who provided so much important research feedback from which this book grew, heartfelt thanks.

To all of you who know in your heart you have work to do that will make a difference, I encourage you.

Disclaimer

This book is written to teach techniques that balance leadership and management skills. These materials also touch upon subjects which require specialized knowledge such as law, finance, investments, insurance, and accounting. Betty Derricott does not hold herself out as having expertise in these specialized fields. The examples provided in this book are to be used in conjunction with your entire team of professional advisors. You are encouraged to seek advice from other consultants in their specialized fields. Compliance with federal and state labor laws are the responsibility of each employer.

All of the cases and examples in this book are taken from real experiences. The names have been changed to protect the privacy of individuals involved.

FOREWORD

by David Moline

It is indeed a privilege and a pleasure to be asked to write the foreword for this powerful, much-needed book.

During my private practice career, I had the great good fortune to work with the author in a group practice. At the time, and even before I recognized the significant importance of leadership training for dentists, Betty was blazing new trails in teamwork for the staff and dentists in the group.

Since that time years ago, I have come to truly appreciate the frontiers that Betty has opened. As an academic dentist, I know that there are very few, if any, curriculum hours in U.S. dental schools devoted to leadership training for dentists. Most unfortunately, very few dental educators recognize that without this basic building block in the curriculum, all of the advanced technological and scientific education may go for naught if the student/ dentist is not first educated in how best to use that technical training.

It therefore becomes somewhat of a "crap shoot" whether the young graduate will ever realize his or her true potential as both a highly educated dentist and as a person with awesome responsibilities to self, staff, patients, and the community. Far too many dentists spend their lives never reaching their true personal and professional potential.

The great pity is that this subject and this book are not part of the curriculum of every U.S. dental school. And even sadder from my perspective is that so very few dental educators realize the tremendous importance of this subject. Surely, this is a reflection on their corporate lack of experience in the private sector of health care.

But, the great good news is that Betty *has* put together this mighty book and attendant courses to help those in practice who recognize the need for help and guidance in this very important subject.

So, from all of us out here in the real world, grateful thanks, Betty, for your tremendous dedication to this task. We really appreciate you!

David O. Moline, DDS, is professor emeritus of the University of Iowa College of Dentistry. He has been awarded fellowship in the American College of Dentists, The Academy of General Dentistry, and the American Association of Hospital Dentists. One of the few dentists to serve on the Board of Regents for the National Library of Medicine, Dr. Moline also served as president of the Academy of General Dentistry in 1976. He is a widely-published author and presenter.

Besides his academic credentials, Dr. Moline spent many years in private practice.

INTRODUCTION

The Twenty-first Century holds before us the certainties of accelerating technological advancements, a global economy, and a cultural shift that boggles the imagination.

Virtual reality will propel us beyond our boundaries. The electronic prowess of our children will challenge the superiority of adulthood. Those of us who are conditioned in the "way things were" will be required to unlearn limiting beliefs. We will be challenged to become like children – willing to explore new possibilities.

In the vacuum of transition where the old way is obsolete and the new way hasn't taken form yet, we will experience feelings of confusion and loss.

While we are learning to shop "on-line" with our personal computers, discovering new ways to do things, we will need some place to attach our anchor or we may feel adrift. We will realize how little of the world around us we can control.

To stay "alive," we will need to know better who we are. We will need to look inside ourselves seeking our core values. We will learn to listen to our hearts and to trust our intuitions.

Business principles will move from quick-fix, competitive strategies to cooperation generated by common values. Success will be measured by satisfaction of work experience, accomplishment, and making a difference. Profitability alone will not drive us any longer. When we become *free to lead,* prosperity will follow us in abundance.

Already, we are beginning to understand that all things are interrelated and that no one can operate in isolation. We are moving toward an *inter-dependent*, global society.

Our desire to become whole is evident in the marketplace. Individuals of all ages, genders, and income levels are becoming involved in aerobics, health food, self-improvement, creative process, and learning to balance the stresses in their lives. We want and deserve personal fulfillment and peace of mind.

We have progressed from the industrialized era of machines to a technological era which mandates advancement of our human consciousness. ***Dentistry, like any other business, must evolve with the changing times and culture.*** We must redefine our businesses to be congruent with our times and our values.

Now, we have the opportunity to lead our profession from the extremes of autocratic rule (benevolent dictatorship) or passive peacekeeping, to a middle ground where authentic human beings are capable of creating more healing, professional environments.

You cannot lead where you have not been. No longer can you grow your practice without growing as a human being. No longer can you preach health (and be believed) without being healthy.

Over the last 20 years, the dentist has been the technical/analytical component of the dental practice, while team members have provided the nurturing intuitive ingredient. Dentists across the country commend dental assistants and hygienists for their nurturing qualities in dealing with people.

In contrast, dentists, coming from linear, analytical training, often despair in their challenge to deal with people, or to "manage" them. Likewise, staff members often express frustration at the divergent approaches of staff and dentist. The professional women who make up dental teams are asking for leadership from the dentists.

In the dental profession this power struggle continues not only between hygienists and dentists, but also between specialists and general practitioners, and, sadly, between providers who mistakenly believe they are in competition with each other.

The need for cooperation is critical. Imagine how the dental profession would be if we all supported and empowered each other.

I have been blessed to work in the profession of dentistry for over 30 years. I have been in the front row of the industry-wide drama that is unfolding in work relationships, management theory, and the balancing of the analytical and creative natures that we all possess.

I am in the business of "growing up" teams of people. I have been privileged to coach dental teams from dependence (how to) up the maturity ladder to independence (responsibility) and to inter-dependence (win/win/win cooperation).

I have seen the power that is released when a group of people becomes a highly energized team. The distinction is not only success in practice growth and profitability, but also in quality and excellence of the work provided.

FREE TO LEAD provides the opportunity to experience self-empowerment. It enables you to identify beliefs that limit your freedom. As you use this doctor's guide to profitable leadership performance, you will work through various processes that are designed to free you from limiting perceptions.

Personal power is defined by choice. The more fully you choose to participate in the exercises provided, the more fully you will recognize the keys to your own success.

HOW TO USE FREE TO LEAD

This material has been tested in small group studies with dentists participating in over 1400 hours of training. Testing has shown that the most powerful results occur consistently from *personal insight.* Therefore, I strongly encourage you to go through the processes as outlined in *Free to Lead.*

For best use of this book:

- Use a spiral-bound notebook for your notes and reflections.
- Use your daily planner to allocate time to work through this guide.
- Follow the outline of the book which is designed to layer the concepts from the inside out.
- Use the chapter self-checks to monitor your progress.
- Using this book, join a study group of about five dentists to meet monthly, focusing on one chapter at a time.

Welcome to the journey!

ADDITIONAL APPLICATIONS

- ✓ For personalized coaching appointments or information on *Free to Lead* small group trainings call Derricott Dental Management at 1-800-756-6613.
- ✓ If you are interested in becoming an authorized facilitator of Authentic Leadership Certification, send a cover letter with your resumé to Derricott Dental Management, 6975 S.W. Sandburg, Suite 130-7, Tigard, Oregon 97223.
- ✓ Printed materials for effective coaching, and personnel development files can be ordered using the order blanks in the back of this book.

1. CHALLENGING THE STATUS QUO

"The dominant principle of organization has shifted, from management in order to control an enterprise, to leadership in order to bring out the best in people and to respond quickly to change."

– *John Naisbitt and Patricia Aburdene,* Megatrends 2000

Each autumn the call of Canada geese lifts my eyes to their graceful formation in the sky. The flock seems to agree on the direction, and the forceful leader breaks through the wind for the many who follow in a V behind. Mates for life, the geese travel together, nurture their young, and rotate leadership as they uplift the rest to soar with ease. All healthy adult geese appear willing to lead. When one is injured, its mate and another pair stay behind. It seems that they all must know how to lead.

While human beings don't have the genetic makeup to fly south every winter, we do have powerful and unique, though perhaps untapped, abilities to lead.

In dental practices, direction is defined by the leader, the dentist. To be *free to lead,* we first must know where we are going.

Lecture circuit speakers have a variety of preferences for dental practices from big to small and from quality-focus to profit-focus. In the last analysis, the only useful strategy for practice success comes from consistent, responsible action implemented by the business owner. It requires leadership to take action that challenges the status quo.

In the face of a changing marketplace and national health care, it is important that we recalibrate our professional compasses.

Let's take a look at how society has changed and dentistry along with it.

HISTORICAL OVERVIEW

What was happening ...

... in society ...	**... in dentistry ...**
... during the agricultural era	
Focus on survival needs	Dentists relived pain, pulled teeth, made dentures
... during the industrial era	
Time was related to productivity	"Fix it" attitudes developed
First clocks and assembly lines	The doctor "fixed" the patient
Problems solved by deductive reasoning based on facts and conclusions	Technology to fill teeth
	Focus on technical efficiency
... during the post-industrial era	
Service-based, information age	Focus on technology and behavior
Human potential movement	• Prevention
Focus on quality	• Home-care education
Problems solved by inductive reasoning based on principles and feelings	Development of health care team including the client in
	• Choice
	• Values
	• Communication
	• Health/Fitness/Wellness

WHERE HAVE WE BEEN?

■ In the agricultural era, in the beginning of dentistry, the focus was to meet fundamental survival needs. Dentists extracted teeth, made dentures, and often traveled about the countryside to relieve pain.

■ The industrial era brought with it the technology to fix teeth. The "Doctor" had all the answers. Patients were in need, and, therefore, *dependent* on the dentist to take care of them.

■ By around 1950, dental practices were small offices with one dentist and usually one "girl." Autocratic management of employees and patients worked very well. There was no dental insurance. Patients paid in cash and bartered for services.

■ By the 1960s, technology had given us the high-speed handpiece. The amount of dentistry we could do increased, while the demand decreased. Government-funded studies indicated a high need for dentistry based on studies of children's tooth decay and missing teeth. With larger educational subsidies, more dentists graduated in the 1970s.

■ Then came dental insurance. In the '80s dentistry doubled its capacity to deliver services with more chairs, more staff members, and more focus on prevention. Patient education became the focus. Patients were included as participants in dental health. Patients began to be more *independent* in regard to their responsibility for home care. Staff members became more independent in specialized skills and their contribution to the profession.

WHERE ARE WE NOW?

The maturity ladder on page 9 illustrates the cultural transition we find ourselves in today. Dental patients have become very discriminating about the quality, the costs, the safety, and the results of services. They are no longer dependent on the doctor to tell them what to do. Many have taken responsibility for prevention, but most still feel dependent upon dental insurance for the finest dental care.

Dentistry in the 1990s requires excellence in technical, behavioral, and organizational skills. Many people have experienced the results of Deming's total quality management[1] in their workplaces. They have come to expect excellence. We must communicate *our* commitment to excellence through highly skilled team members, including the dentists, who themselves are intentionally moving up the maturity ladder.

Taking such responsibility means being able to respond constructively to change. Before we can enjoy the freedom of *interdependent* relationships, we need to reexamine current perceptions of management and leadership.

THE BALANCE OF LEADERSHIP

In the American work culture, bosses often are viewed as autocratic bullies who are self-centered and interested mostly in money. On the other hand, employees are seen as selfish, hard to motivate, defensive, and devisive.[2] In the face of this cultural bias we have to build cooperative teamwork. It is a challenge to every kind of business.

Working in dentistry for over 30 years, I have experienced many styles of management. I have seen the very ***autocratic*** doctor

---

[1]W. Edwards Deming offered direction for the transformation of American-style business management in *Out of Crisis,* published in 1986 by the Massachusetts Institute of Technology Center for Advanced Engineering Study.

[2]Ryan and Oestreich, *Driving Fear Out of the Workplace,* 1991.

COMMUNICATION PATTERNS

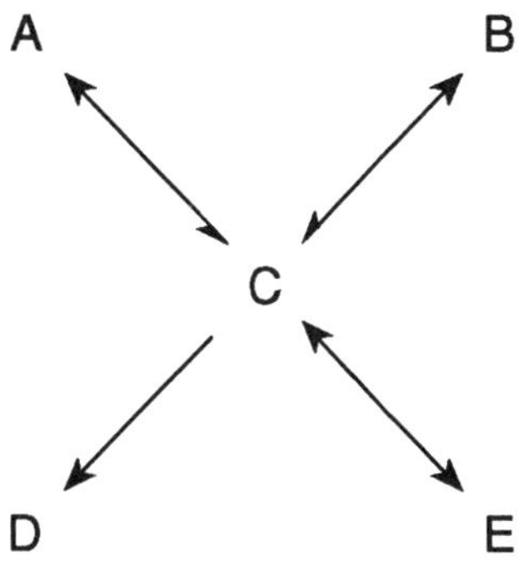

Autocratic

- Faster communication
- Members bored
- Hostility toward leader
- Ineffective with complex learning tasks
- Unable to cope with stress

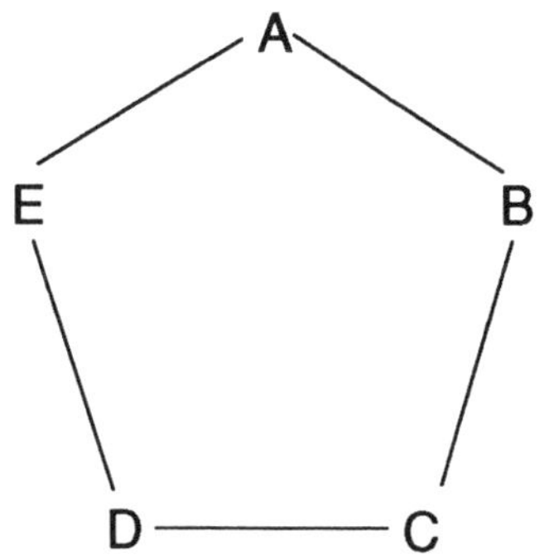

Democratic

- Slow - inaccurate, but "happy"
- No leader
- No systematic approach to problem solving
- More skill with learning tasks
- Accommodates stress better

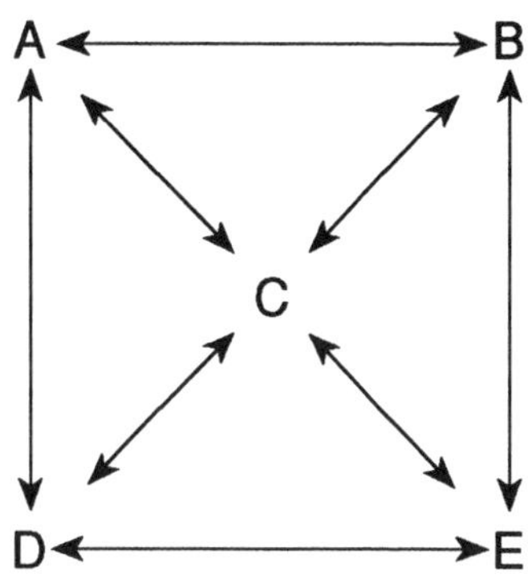

Participative

- C's function is facilitator
- Responds openly, non-judgmentally
- Members secure in offering opinions
- Members learn tasks with efficiency (even under stress)
- Committed to achieving group goals for which they feel ownership

Blanchard-Hersey Study, 1973.

who tells everyone what to do, when to do it, how to do it, and then looks over the shoulder to make sure it was done that way. This can be successful when the employees are highly dependent on direction. At least expectations are clear. Staff members who need more autonomy will leave. The probable consequence of this style of management is a high turnover of staff members, lack of creativity, boredom, and mediocrity. In such a practice growth is limited because of the limits of one person. Dependent patients will be attracted to this practice.

Much more often I see ***democratic leadership,*** which I call "country club management." Many dentists need to feel liked. In an effort to be socially acceptable, no real communication takes place. Often people in this environment keep quiet and put on a phony smile to cover disappointment and displeasure. Without a way to clear up misunderstandings, resentment and frustration spread like a disease. This is not a healthy environment. It models dependence on others for approval. The doctor and staff members who are dependent on patient approval lose control of the business. Accounts receivable and broken appointments are symptoms of this management style.

Participative management, on the other hand, provides for delegation, open group interaction, and feedback with accountability. Under this style of management, team members have the opportunity to contribute to the leadership process.

Leadership skills begin to develop with participative management. Both the autocratic leader and the democratic leader can successfully make the shift to participative management.

The leadership process balances content with context, jobs with people, tasks with results. For example:

- A *content* statement: "I have a high producing practice with a profit of $200,000 per year."

- A *context* statement: "I have peace of mind and satisfaction in my work."

BALANCE BECOMES A LEADERSHIP PROCESS

CONTENT	CONTEXT
DETAIL	VISION
CIRCUMSTANCE	CHANGE
TACTICS/STRATEGIES	VALUES
TASKS	RESULTS
JOBS	PEOPLE

When things don't work, leaders change the variables. This means keeping the big picture of their vision in focus while allowing team members to fine-tune the details.

WHAT'S THE DIFFERENCE?

Let us distinguish between management and leadership. **Management** relates to the analytical organization of tasks and action. **Leadership** is the soul, the spirit, the intrinsic values.

Leadership is the personal contribution of the leader to the process of management.

Management = Doing	**Leadership = Being**
setting goals	pursues their passion
giving reports	visionary – inspiring
forecasting	advocates mission, values, beliefs
analyzing	walks the talk – demonstrates values
motivating	clear with expectations
delegating	rewarding results
evaluating	allows motivation from within
coordinating	encouraging – coach
making decisions	good listener
providing tools	empowers others
providing resources	flexible
providing time and energy	takes risks – allows mistakes
providing money	respects intuition
providing equipment	ability to focus
managing use of resources	catalyst

President Eisenhower once defined leadership as "the art of getting someone else to do something you want done because he wants to do it."

In order to sell quality dentistry, we create value for our service which results in our patients *wanting to do* the treatment. The logical prerequisite is having a team that *wants to do the dentistry.* This includes whatever it takes to implement shared goals that express the team's shared values.

THE CHALLENGE OF INTER-DEPENDENCE

Life is by nature inter-dependent. As humans, and as team members, we begin by being ***dependent***. We are dependent upon others to produce desired results, upon the approval/validation of others, and upon others' thinking. Slowly we move up the maturity ladder to being ***independent***. We become accountable for results. Finally, team members become ***inter-dependent***. Inter-dependence is an attitude of appreciation for how much we all need each other. We look for the best in each other and encourage pro-active thinking. Rather than reacting into crisis management, team members become creative at organizing life around their priorities. In the case of a dental team that means organizing tasks around the values of the team.

As individuals we "grow" up the ladder; as leaders and team members we grow up; and as a society we are being required to grow up.

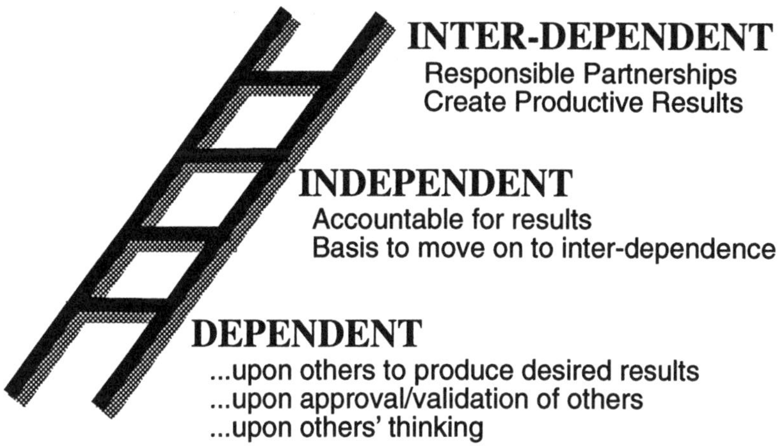

LIFE IS BY NATURE INTER-DEPENDENT[3]

---

[3]The concept of the maturity continuum is discussed throughout *The Seven Habits of Highly Effective People* by Stephen R. Covey, specifically on pages 48-49. This book is recommended for study in conjunction with *Free to Lead.*

In the 1960s Marshall McLuhan foresaw the world becoming a "global village," and he was right. In many ways the world is turning into a small town and society is becoming more global. Along with this comes more and more change, taking us tumbling with it as we struggle to retain some sense of balance. Issues around health care, the environment, nuclear disarmament, bioengineering, political coalitions, and conflicts all have sped up into a kind of chaos.

Amid this, we face a collective challenge to make the right choices. We are being asked to respond to urgent situations all around us.

Like it or not, change has grabbed us. We might as well participate in choosing the direction it takes us. Everyone may not agree on a direction or a solution, but even a small group with a common vision can make a big difference guiding change. That is what leaders and teams do.

The alternative is feeling *out of control* in times of change. It is ironic that we must let go of what we have to grab on to something better. In between we experience the void which is the uncharted water between the safe, familiar harbor and the new world we seek.

It's a paradigm shift. You and I are being asked to embrace new ways of seeing the world, from quantum physics to the communications super-highway. Hang on to your hat!

Business has not been spared. For business management the new paradigm says that our greatest resource is *human potential.* In order to transform this potential into energy and action, we must create a new environment within our organizations – one where human beings can grow and develop.

The status quo is being challenged. You are being challenged. In many ways it comes down to the message, "Lead, follow, or get out of the way!"

機

The Chinese figure for the word "crisis" is written as a combination of the symbols for "danger" and "opportunity."

Workplace crises over demands for higher wages, fair benefits, and respect are often seen as gender issues. All too often, these demands escalate into an adversarial dynamic of men against women, dentist against staff.

From such a crisis our opportunity lies in creating an environment in the workplace where we can move past adversarial behavior to develop a co-creative, inter-dependent team.

The costs will become insurmountable if we continue to deny the need for this change. The consequences of undeveloped human potential are fear, anger, judgment, and separation which result in stress, broken relationships, sickness, and death of the organization.

Developed human potential leads to creativity, growth, acceptance, and belonging, resulting in a cohesive, productive, profitable team.

Put in these terms, the choice is clear.

DEVELOPING HUMAN POTENTIAL

We have the foundation to reach higher levels of human potential than ever before. Abraham Maslow's hierarchy shows the stages of need that must be fulfilled for humans to reach their potential or "self-actualization."

Self-actualization:

♦ Becoming more and more of what one is.
♦ To become everything one is capable of becoming.
♦ Enjoyment of *being.*

THE PROCESS OF HUMAN DEVELOPMENT

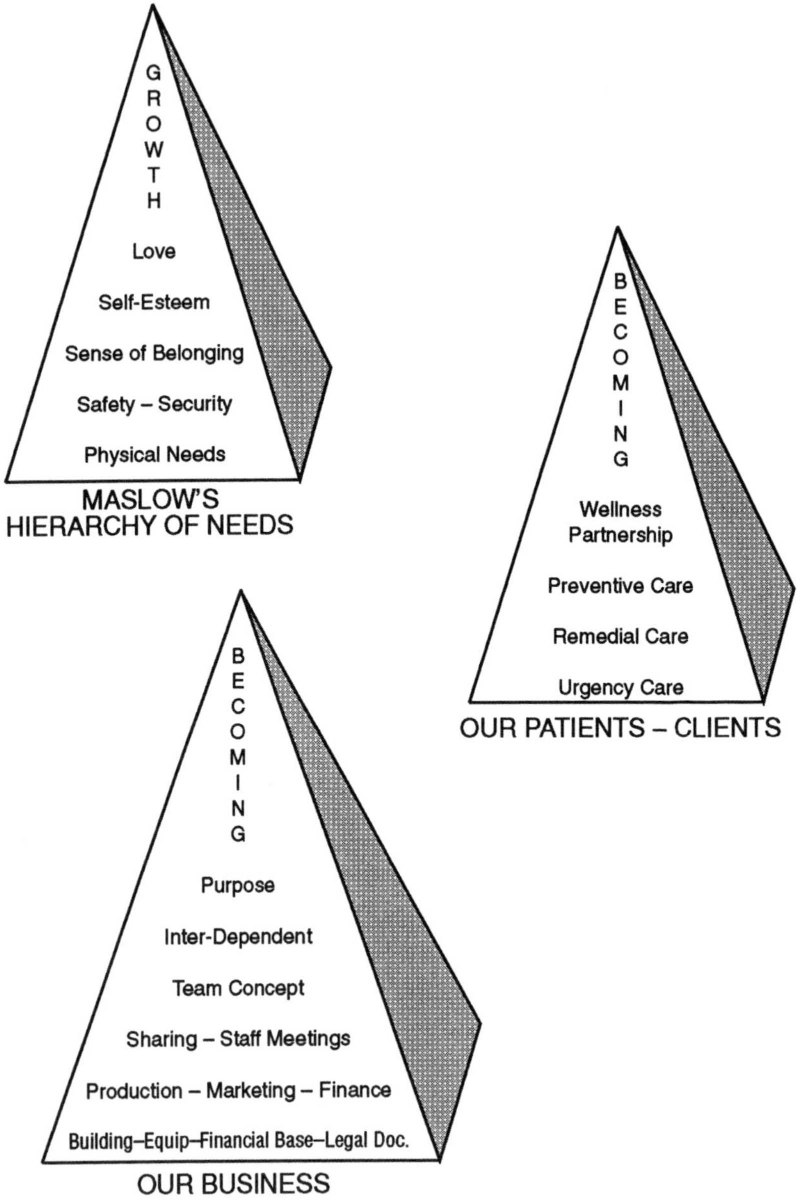

The end result will be an environment where every person – dentist, employee, and patient – can exist in a state of *becoming*. As we grow healthy humans by fulfilling first their physical and safety needs, then by providing a sense of belonging, self-esteem, and love; so we grow our dental practices by taking care of basic physical needs first and then moving toward team inter-dependence. We grow our patients by taking care of their immediate pain, preventing future problems, and developing a partnership for good dental health. Over and over again we see the theme of the maturity ladder.

To create an environment of inter-dependence:

❶ The dentist(s) must choose how they will relate to associates, employees, and patients.

❷ Having chosen, the dentist(s) must share what they want with staff and allow staff members to decide if it matches their own vision.

❸ Staff members should be *free to choose* the options with which they will be comfortable. This means that they develop within the vision of the dentist *or,* seeing that their values are not compatible with those of the dentist, they are free to find a more compatible environment elsewhere.

❹ The dentist and staff together develop a method to relate their values to each other and to their patients.

❺ Educational aids for patients (philosophy pamphlets, wellness options, printed material, visual/auditory, kinesthetic models) can relate the values, options, and probable consequences of dental care, so patients, too, can be *free to choose.*

WHAT DO WE WANT?

What do staff members want? What do doctors, assistants, hygienists, business staff want? Is it possible to reach agreement?

In June of 1990, I did a survey asking dental team members about their perceptions of the most rewarding and the most stressful aspects of their jobs. Responses from women working in chairside assisting, business offices, and dental hygiene are listed in order from the most to the least:

Administrative Assistants

Most rewarding:	Most stressful:
Accomplishment	Doctor communication
Respect	Patient communication
Patient relations	Scheduling
Good boss	Team communication
Staff relations	Interruptions
Money	Recall/collections/insurance

Chairside Assistants

Most rewarding:	Most stressful:
Staff relations	Dealing with doctor
Patient relations	Dealing with schedule
Good boss	Working as a team
Accomplishment	Dealing with patients
Respect	Lab work
Money	No breaks
Helping people/learning/ 4-day week/good hours	Health hazards/meeting goals

Hygienists

Most rewarding:	Most stressful:
Good boss/good dentistry	Dealing with patients
Accomplishment	Dealing with doctor
Money	Dealing with staff

Patient relations	Paperwork
Respect	The clock
Staff relations	Lack of control over earnings
Work schedule (freedom)	Professional liability, hazards

Asked what they would change about their job or their profession if they could change *just one thing*, all groups responded with "better team communication." They included a change or improvement of attitude referred to as "professional attitude." Other responses had to do with features of the facility such as adequate space, updated decor, and pleasant surroundings.

The following survey was done with graduating Authentic Leadership Certification doctors.

Doctors in Leadership

Most rewarding:	**Most stressful:**
Financial security	Achieving financial security
Seeing patients get healthy	Days that don't work
Appreciation expressed by patients, staff, and peers	Being behind schedule
	PMS
Knowing I have the ability to help	The schedule
A happy staff	The staff
Seeing staff members mature	The responsibilities
When the day "works	Difficult patients
A sense of completion for the day	Lack of skills to deal with
Learning and growth	organizing, managing, leading

Based on the information from this survey, it is no wonder that dentists and team members working in the same office day after day bypass each other in communication. We could learn so much from each other if we really were willing to get outside of our own biases and listen to each other's perspective.

LEARNING TO LISTEN

Find out what your team members need by asking them!

Exercise: This assignment is an experiment in intentional listening between you and your team members. Remember that for your team members to talk to you, they need to feel safe and to understand your purpose.

This probably is a new behavior for you, so, before you begin, explain what you are doing. For example, say to your team member, "I have an assignment for my leadership study to learn to listen. I have been asked to interview you to practice really hearing. Will you please take a few minutes to answer some questions?"

If you feel that a volatile subject such as raises may come up, make it safe for both of you to discuss it by saying, "My intention is to hear your concerns and feelings as accurately as possible. I will not make any decisions or solve any problems today, but we will decide on the next step of action."

The following outline will help you develop the skill of intentional listening. ***This is the most important leadership skill you can learn.*** Like any of the technical skills you have learned to be a good dentist, listening requires daily focus and daily practice. The benefits of hearing another person, whether that person is an employee, patient, or business associate, will empower you to be a good leader.

Steps for Intentional Listening

❶ Ask questions.

❷ Focus on the answers.

❸ Use interested body language, eye contact, nod, smile, lean forward.

❹ Ask more *open-ended* questions using "why" or "when."

- "Do you feel frustrated?" (Calls for a "Yes/No" response and is, therefore, a *closed-ended* question.)
- "Why do you feel frustrated? (Calls for some exploring and more dialogue and is an *open-ended* question.)
- "Anything else?" (Also an *open-ended* question.)

❺ Use feedback, get clarification, and check accuracy
- "So what you really appreciate is ________?"
- "If I heard you correctly, you believe ________."

❻ Stay open, seeking continued dialogue, by asking such questions as:
- "How can I help?"
- "What shall we do?"
- "What are your requests?"

❼ Closure: Get an agreement on any action to be taken, or agreement that no action will be taken.
- Decide now. (80 percent of decisions can be made now.)
- Defer decision with date to decide.
- Be clear about your next step.

LISTEN UP! This is the most important skill you can learn. You already do it every day. You listen to team members and you listen to patients.

Remember to *consider your staff members as your first line of clients.* Your second line of clients are your patients. The quality of service provided for your first line of clients will directly determine the quality of service provided to your second line of clients, and ultimately will determine your success.

Listen intentionally. Practice every day. Watch your entire team learn more effective listening skills. Videotape new patient consultations. See how well you are listening. Seeing yourself allows you to refine your skills.

Healing requires hearing.

WHAT DO TEAM MEMBERS WANT FROM A LEADER?

Over 1,400 hours of research reveals these common-sense, yet often neglected, requests. These comments are from staff members just like yours. These are some of the things they want from you, their leader:

1. *When I ask for a decision that only you can make, tell me now* <u>*or*</u> *tell me the date I can expect your answer.*
2. *Keep your commitment to make decisions when you said you would.*
3. *When I ask for time to talk to you about a problem, make time to REALLY LISTEN.*
4. *When I tell you about the problem, please don't tell me how to fix it! Listen, ask questions, understand me. Ask me, "How can I best support you to get this problem solved?"*
5. *Acknowledge my accomplishments. Say thank you.*
6. *Include me by asking my opinion, especially when I will be directly affected by the decision.*
7. *Make sure I understand your expectations, so I know when I am successful.*
8. *Respect me as a partner in your business. What happens matters to me, too!*
9. *Be loyal to me and stand up for me. Speak well of me to others.*
10. *Speak to me honestly and directly about how I can do better. Believe in me and keep challenging me to learn.*
11. *Thank you for asking me what I want and need!*

CHAPTER 1: SELF-CHECK

- ❏ I have practiced active listening with at least one team member. What I learned:

- ❏ I have gathered information about what followers expect from their leaders. What I learned:

- ❏ Consider the concepts of the maturity ladder.

  As a leader, I am: dependent ______ %
  independent ______ %
  inter-dependent ______ %

  As a work team, we are:
  dependent (exhibit blaming attitudes) ______ %
  independent (accountable for results) ______ %
  inter-dependent (co-creative) ______ %

  Our patients are:
  dependent (urgency- or remedial-motivated) ______ %
  independent (accountable, pre-appointed) ______ %
  inter-dependent (partners in health, referring new patients, excited about dental health benefits) ______ %

2. INNER MANAGEMENT

"There are three things extremely hard:
steel, diamond, and to know one's self."

– Ben Franklin

Successful management of tasks and leadership of people require the solid foundation of self-confidence, self-esteem, and congruence. How you perform depends on your own personal beliefs and values.

If you are to lead, be the first member of your team to embark on the experience of introspective self-analysis. As the leader, clarify expectations of yourself, with yourself, before you ask staff members to engage in clarifying expectations with you. Lead the way.

The more you learn about this process of inner management the better you will be at supporting others. You cannot *manage* other people, but you can create an environment where other people manage themselves to achieve the results you both desire.

Vision, mission, and *purpose* are the ingredients to effective leadership. A personal vision is essential.

To help you reach the source of your vision, let's go back to another place and another time through the paradox of the puzzle.

THE PARADOX OF THE PUZZLE

I shook the box, wrapped brightly for me
with red paper and green ribbon, and under the tree.
It was a game of some kind, the noises disclosed,
a wonderful challenge for my mind, I supposed.

Eager to play, I ripped open the paper,
revealing a plain cardboard box!
The game inside, a puzzle all right,
with pieces so many, so tiny, I wondered with fright,
How many puzzles are mixed up in here?
What is the picture the game will make clear?
What is the purpose in this mess?
A dirty joke at my expense?
A personal challenge?
An endurance test?

Abstract diversion.
No picture to guide me.
No directions, no user manual, no guarantee?
Just like life, the freedom to be!

Life, like a box of puzzle pieces, comes with a picture of how it is supposed to be. We hold that picture in our mind not noticing how the pieces change each day. We struggle to fit all the pieces together, forcing and pounding them into place to keep the picture as it "should" be. Throwing away the old box cover with the outdated picture, while saving the pieces as possibilities, opens us up to creating our own unique picture of life.

Resources available to us contain puzzle pieces for every conceivable picture. We are *free to create* our own picture.

A LOOK AT THE PAST

We know that the past is not our potential and that we are not limited by the past, but let's look back for reference because our core beliefs were created there.

■ The power of vision worked, at least once in Dr. Bridge's life. He had a vision when he chose a career in dentistry. He didn't say, "I will try out dental school. Maybe I'll graduate. Maybe someday I'll have a practice *if* I pass the boards!" Why not?

Dr. Bridge trained with conviction and commitment. The price was too high, the vision too real, the possibilities too big to enter with half-hearted expectations.

What was your own motivation then? Was it to be your own boss? Was it the freedom of being in charge of your own schedule? Was it the possibility of profit? Was it the high social esteem associated with your degree? How about enhancing your technical skill? Freedom, autonomy, respect, and financial independence are common answers. This may be a significant piece of your puzzle to save as possibility.

There was so much Dr. Bridge didn't know when he started school! He came through fine, but not unscathed. The regimen of linear learning was driving and demanding. His emotions were not important in the analytical transfer of information and technical skill. Dr. Bridge tightened his self-discipline and determination, and made it through test after test, obstacle after obstacle.

That initial vision of an idyllic career in dentistry may have been pushed aside for "have to," "got to," or "make the grade," but Dr. Bridge made it and you did, too. Like Dr. Bridge, you walked across the stage and you were a doctor.

Congratulations!

■ There was so much Dr. Fillings didn't know. There were school debts. Getting a practice started meant more debts. The student's "someday struggle" continued.

Did Dr. Fillings have a vision then? A picture of how his practice might look? Was it difficult for him without a clearly outlined, linear model of "how to" for his practice? There was no formula like there had been in training.

Not knowing how to build a practice could have meant disgrace and failure. Dr. Fillings criticized himself for not being quite good enough. And he felt isolated.

Is isolation a puzzle piece in your picture? Do you sometimes feel like it is you against them? "Them" might be the school, the banker, the equipment salesman, the insurance company, the economy, the employees, the patients. Were "they" irresponsible? Were there failed appointments, unpaid bills?

There were plenty of "how to" books, tapes, seminars, and articles. Dr. Fillings devoured them seeking office success. Fear of failure was his driving energy.

Dr. Fillings went to every continuing education course he could find. He got some formulas and some answers. He took notes and went back to the office. He told employees how to do it right. (Now that felt good!) It was exciting to take some action. It was a start.

Dr. Fillings had some pieces that worked. His favorite speaker made it work. He went to hear her every time she was in town.

Over the years, the "How To" checklist grew:

- ❑ Management consultants can fix it. Hire one, a good one, and be on the leading edge.
- ❑ Buy a practice.
- ❑ Sell a practice.
- ❑ Enroll in a PPO.

- ❑ Free exams, mass mailing, effective recall, chart audits, monitors, GOALS.
- ❑ Management by objective.
- ❑ Raise your fees, reduce your fees, keep a loss leader.
- ❑ Sell the accounts receivable and let somebody else worry about them!

In a state of confusion, Dr. Fillings decided to focus on technical skill and hope for the best.

■ Dr. Crown finally achieved some success! He was able to put his worries behind.

Do you remember how it was when you really started making money?

Finally, Dr. Crown seemed to be doing all right. The amount of money that flowed through his bank account was mind-boggling! After all those years of struggle, he deserved to have a good time. His spouse and family were ready for this new life-style. They bought a new house. Dr. Crown needed a toy, so he bought a boat. His credit was good and his life was fine.

Do you remember this feeling of abundance?

Meanwhile, it took a year for Dr. Crown to pay last year's taxes and he is behind already on this year's taxes. Cash flow is 30 to 60 days behind and work isn't fun any more. How could prosperity pass by so quickly? There is not enough to go around. The more Dr. Crown gets, the more he needs. "Work harder," he tells himself. This isn't a very bright picture.

BEYOND THE PAST

Author and futurist Marilyn Ferguson gives a wonderful analogy of how we react to painful experiences. "When we're born, she says, "we have a vast space in our mind, like a huge castle. In the process of life, we experience pain in one of the rooms and, out of fear, we close off the room. One by one, we close off the rooms, until we find ourselves living in the broom closet. It is very stuffy in there!"

In the broom closet there isn't much room for vision. There's hardly room to breath. But we are adaptable. We get accustomed to the limited space. Here are some typical remarks made from the broom closet by dentists.

- "I'm trapped doing dentistry."
- "The bureaucrats are in control."
- "Insurance companies have our hands tied."
- "There are too many dentists; not enough business to go around."
- "Overhead is too high."
- "We can't make money. Ask anybody at society meetings!"
- "People can't afford it."

You may or may not have had these experiences. They are examples of puzzle pieces that limit us.

When we allow our logical, linear, analytical thinking to become negative and to take over, it blocks creativity and resists change. As a consequence, we become trapped in "circumstance." We don't have to avoid being logical, but we should realize how limiting it is to be dominated by negative thoughts. They shut out the light of creativity and keep new choices in the shadow.

Computer specialists have identified hundreds of computer virus strains. Our minds, like computers, can become flawed through the virus of insidious, self-generating fear. Fear of failure, fear of change, and fear of rejection. Free-floating fear. We can identify these puzzle pieces of fear and discard them.

There is another way to view limiting circumstance. Napoleon Hill wrote about it in *Think and Grow Rich*, first published in 1937. Desire leads to thoughts which lead to energy which leads to action. Stated another way, what you think is what you are. Desire, thoughts, energy, and action are all within your power to control. They are the foundation upon which you can realize the picture you have seen, designed, and created. *Today, you can choose the picture you really want.*

BACK TO THE PRESENT

We easily become anchored in our experience and replay our past. If the past is not what we want in the future, we must be *open to change.* This is why I employ coaches and facilitators for myself and my work. I take deliberate steps to associate with groups of people who have similar values, who can draw out my positive thinking and influence me to take action.

Environment is stronger than will. Surround yourself with affirming people and enriching experiences.

It takes great courage to move beyond what we know. It also takes great patience. We have been accustomed to having all the answers. That feels safe. This process of creating new ideas, however, is outside the objective realm of answers.

The present holds the possibility for change. In the present we have the opportunity to examine where we are now, and to explore new possibilities. We are *free to lead.*

EXERCISES

The following exercises will help clarify your values. They are puzzle pieces that have been missing from our educational process. They call upon the intuitive, creative self to lead beyond preprogrammed actions and to rid us of the mind virus.

Get out your notebook. As you think about the questions, set aside the need to know "how." There are no "right" answers. Delay your judgment of new ideas.

Vision: Time Future

Imagine yourself on the day you retire.

As I lock the office door for the last time and pass the baton of leadership on to another, I feel:

I truly can say I am proud:

I regret:

If I could do it over again, I would:

The most memorable experiences of my career were when:

Doctor Questionnaire

Why did you choose dentistry as your life's work?

Are you happy that you did?

What elements of dentistry are dissatisfiers for you?

What are the elements of dentistry that you enjoy?

How do you see your staff members in relation to your practice of dentistry?

How would you define the value of the service you render to your patients (clients)?

Adversity Process

Everything in my professional practice would be perfect except for: (Or, if I were buying this practice, what would I change?)

Adversity Process Instructions:

- After you answer the question, place an "X" alongside each item that you can change. Place a "Y" alongside each item that you and your team can change. Underline those items that are impossible to change.
- Look at the items marked with an "X." What do you intend to do with them?
- Regarding those marked with a "Y," what is your plan?
- If there are underlined situations, how might you "reframe" them or change your mind about them to achieve the most positive result?

Self Survey

Answer the questions on the following pages in your notebook, as you write down what you want in your life. Then examine your activities and the feeling associated with each of them. Thoughtfully done, this process will help you identify what you want to experience. It gives you the opportunity to clarify your intentions for yourself.

❶ Spend time away from your routines. Go to the ocean or the mountains. Go to a place where you find energy and renewal. Reflect on your life and respond to the questions posed by this process.

❷ On the way listen to music that inspires you. See things that uplift you.

❸ Write from your feelings, not only from your mind.

Obstacle: You may try to talk yourself out of this process. You may say, "I don't have time for this foolishness!" You may be very uncomfortable with the "feeling" process. In order to become a balanced, fully-living, whole human being, you need to experience your feelings so you can learn to balance your analytical skills with your creative skills. There is no shortcut. There is no map. You have to create your own.

Obstacle: The next argument from the analytical side of your brain may be: "I can't do this leadership stuff, it sounds too hard. Why don't I just hire a good office manager?" You *can* hire a wonderful office manager who may be very creative and a very intuitive leader. By transferring the leadership role to another person, however, you subject your practice to that person's bias. Your practice will be led by another person's values, principles, and integrity, not your own. Are you really willing to give up that leadership role?

Personal Intentions

In my profession I intend to:

If I were to accomplish what I have listed above, I would feel...

In my professional relationships I intend to:

If I were to accomplish what I have listed above, I would feel...

In my family and personal relationship I intend to:

If I were to accomplish what I have listed above, I would feel...

In my community, social, and global perspective I intend to:

If I were to accomplish what I have listed above, I would feel...

In regard to my self-care, I intend to:

Physical Emotional Spiritual

Values Assessment

If I had the *time* to do anything I wanted to do, I would:

If I had the *money* to do anything I wanted to do, I would:

In the last 10 days I spent my time:

Activity	Approximate Hours	Feeling Associated

In the last 10 days I spent my money on:

Activity	Approximate $ Amount	Feeling Associated

What do I want to experience more of?

What do I want to experience less of?

How can I fill myself with pleasure and joy?

CONSIDER WHY PEOPLE FAIL TO BECOME LEADERS

The leader begins the journey before asking team members to follow. The leader "walks the talk" and provides an example. If, on your journey, you come upon the following obstacles, consider why people fail to become effective leaders.

Obstacle: Lack of clear expectations.
Solution: Decide what you want – really!

Obstacle: Don't know how to lead.
Solution: Make time for learning and practicing leadership skills

Obstacle: Don't know why leadership is important.
Solution: Ask questions – listen – give yourself permission to continue learning.

Obstacle: Won't or don't lead anyway.
Solution: It's a mismatch. Find a new profession or become a follower working for someone else.

CHAPTER 2: SELF-CHECK

- ❑ After completing the Adversity Process I realize those things that can't be changed are:

  Regarding the above, I choose to:

- ❑ I have completed the Values Assessment.
- ❑ I have considered my Personal Intentions.

  With this information and self-assessment, I can:

- ❑ I have defined what I want to experience more and less of.
- ❑ My self-care commitment to myself is:

  Action — Time Frame/Date

- ❑ Write your own personal mission statement.

3. CHOOSING THE VISION

"Companies are propelled by a new kind of synergy when employees are tuned in to a common vision."
— from "The Mystical Corporation," SUCCESS!, *Aug. 1986*

Everything that has ever been invented began with an idea. Not just any idea, but a **big idea**. An inventor sees a finished product in his mind's eye. The picture captures all the senses. Feelings of adventure and excitement lead to the question: "What if ...?"

This describes vision. It goes beyond what we want. It is what we dream of. With a picture in our mind and a passion in our heart, we begin to act like our dreams are reality.

The vision does not have to be earth-shaking. It may be small and simple, but it is *powerful* because it is of *value.*

In your office, the process of defining core values is initiated by you, the leader. Clarifying what you want follows a simple format that can be applied to many situations.

Ask yourself these questions:

❶ What are all the options?

❷ What are the probable beneficial consequences of each option?

❸ Knowing the options and understanding the consequences, *can I choose freely*?

As a decision-making tool, these steps are not new. We always perceive options, anticipate consequences or results of these options, and make our decisions on these insights.

Too often, however, we focus on options to avoid undesirable consequences. With this approach it is easy to create a vision of what we don't want – our energy and activity resulting in what we fear. "This is what I want," is a much more powerful statement than, "This is what I need," or, "This is what I don't want." Recognizing your *freedom to choose action* toward a desired picture will help to focus your vision.

If a magician could wave a magic wand and create whatever you want, what would it be? This is a question *you* must answer. This is the next step, the leap of faith.

> If you continue to act as you've always acted,
> You're going to get what you always got!
>
> If you continue to think as you've always thought,
> You're going to act as you always acted and
> get what you always got!
>
> If you continue to process information the way
> you've always processed information;
> You're going to think what you've always thought,
> Act as you've always acted, and
> Get what you've always got!
>
> – *Marilyn Ferguson*

THE BUY IN

Communicating your *vision and intention* to employees means relating to them what is valuable to you. This also means clarifying the logic behind the value. People respond better when they *understand* how you *feel* about something. Then, they can relate this to how *they feel* about it. Any primer on sales will emphasize that people ultimately buy new products or services based on emotion, how they *feel*, not what they think.

Our basic values are intrinsic to who we are. Therefore, discussing our values can make us feel potentially vulnerable. Our values are very intimate subjects. This may explain our reluctance to clarify deep desires both to ourselves and to our associates. Pushing past that resistance and taking the risk to expose values allows widespread ownership of them by all team members. A successful professional practice cultivates trust and shared values.

> *"We resolutely refuse to follow those who lack confidence in their own beliefs. Confusion over where the leader stands creates stress. We simply do not trust people who will not tell us their values, ethics, and standards." –Kouzes and Posner,* The Leadership Challenge

---

Take a chance. Declare what you really want! Then unconditionally commit to focus every day on your vision. Believe it, declare it, talk about it, and enroll the support of others. This is powerful stuff and it works.

WHAT IS SHOWING UP IN YOUR PRACTICE?

As you review the following checklist, some concerns may become evident. Are any of these showing up in your practice?

- ❑ Staff turnover?
- ❑ Complaints regarding lack of trust?
- ❑ Backed into the corner for more money at every turn?
- ❑ Complaints about lack of appreciation?

- ❑ Excuses and reasons?
- ❑ Too busy to change or learn?
- ❑ "Us" and "Them" attitudes?
- ❑ A lot of talk – no results?
- ❑ Struggle to pay the bills?
- ❑ Just getting by?
- ❑ People just putting in their time?
- ❑ Lack of commitment?
- ❑ Lack of enthusiasm?

You have more power than you know to change these situations. What you see showing up in your practice is a reflection of something you are doing or saying or thinking.

This is *good* news!

Why? Because you have the power to change yourself.

You may have been trying for years to change the behaviors of other people. Give it up! You are powerless to control others. You gain power when you can recognize behaviors that are incongruent with your vision.

So, take another look at the whole picture. Ask yourself what you can change in your own attitudes and behaviors to model what you want.

Attitude Affects Results

In a large practice where two dentists work with the same team members, I asked each dentist to complete the statement, "My staff is __________."

Privately one doctor said, "My staff is wonderful. They are committed. They are creative. They are always involved in making things happen. They are full of enthusiasm and really fun to be with."

When I asked the second dentist the same question of the same staff, his answer was, "My staff is greedy!"

Finally I surveyed team members regarding each dentist. When asked to describe dentist #1, staff members said, "This doctor is enthusiastic, fun to be around, flexible. He is great. We really love him and enjoy working with him."

When asked to describe dentist #2, staff members responded with an overwhelming similarity. They all said in effect, "He's greedy! He is money-hungry. He is never satisfied. He's always demanding. Our work is never good enough. It's not fun working with Dr. #2."

"What you are speaks so loudly, I can't hear what you say." –Ralph Waldo Emerson

---

If we want appreciation, we can create it by being more appreciative. Give what you want to get. If you want your team members to be more time conscious, be more time conscious yourself. Model the desired behavior and acknowledge it in others.

As doctors take more accountability for leadership, they are able to see their own behavior in the reflection of others around them. Chances are good that your staff takes their cue from you. What do you see? What you see is a reflection of what you are. The following true stories will further illustrate this point.

■ Perfectionist Prima Donna

The dentist seems like a prima donna to the scheduling staff when she routinely runs behind schedule and when the order to reschedule patients is the rule rather than the exception. She has no regard for anyone else or their time. She is perceived as irresponsible and unreliable. No wonder it is so hard for her to get staff members to cooperate.

The staff members seem unprofessional to the dentist. They don't follow orders; they talk behind her back; and they seem to be in mutiny. They are always behind and never get the job done.

These two sides go through the day reacting like opponents in a tennis match. They are trying to score a point, rather than to care for the patients. Being right becomes the objective and everyone suffers.

The paradox is that each side is right *and* each side is wrong. The dentist is a perfectionist. In her effort to complete the procedure with perfection, she underestimates the time needed. Her focus on the immediate technical problem obscures the big picture of the whole day which includes the entire schedule, the other patients who will be inconvenienced, and the quality of care. The staff members do not see the detail of the technical procedure requiring the dentist's full attention. The staff members conclude that the dentist is an ego-centered prima donna!

■Caught in the Crossfire

Diana, the business manager, faked a smile as she greeted me for my appointment. A quick scan of the normally impeccable office revealed disorder unlike I had seen there before. Stacks of charts, open drawers, and computer printouts spilling onto the floor made me wonder. Then I saw the doctor's teenage daughter standing timidly by the file cabinet, ducking from view and from Diana's frantic efforts to restore order.

As Diana quickly escorted me past the devastation, she apologized under her breath, "I'm sorry." My compassionate hug was ill-timed, resulting in a cascade of tears and Diana's retreat to the restroom.

Diana is a professional. She is mature and a master of patient relations. The doctor is committed to quality care and a new member of my leadership study group.

Since he already had been introduced to leadership accountability, I did not tiptoe around the obvious. "Good morning, my friend," I greeted him. "What have you done to create this confusion?" He blushed, took a deep breath, and acknowledged that he had a lot to learn about leadership.

From his viewpoint, it was good for his daughter to work around the office, assisting Diana, and helping Diana learn to manage others. From Diana's perspective, the daughter was an untrained hindrance, crowding an already small office space. In order to bridge the gap, he should have asked Diana about hiring his daughter and listened to her response.

The doctor's behavior changed as he learned to slow down, to take a more collaborative approach, and to release the heavy responsibility to "fix it" all alone.

Exercise: The Mirror Test

Here is an opportunity to assess some of your leadership skills in action.

❶ Take out your notebook and make a page heading titled "The Mirror Exercise."

❷ Write down the name of each of your team members, leaving five lines under each name.

❸ Write at least five adjectives that describe each team member. Be thoughtful and deliberate about this process.

❹ Reflect on these questions for each team member:

- What do I do daily to reflect the positive in each person?
- What do I do that may model undesired behaviors?
- What is my intention for each person?
- How can I create a safe place for each person to work?

Create a vision of how you want things to be. Focus on what you want. Model that. Become that. Do that. Now. Every day. With everyone around you.

SETTING YOUR MISSION

A group is not a team until the members have a common purpose. Every team needs a *clearly stated* mission. The mission is the team's statement of purpose. Mission provides direction for achieving goals. It is the map to your destination. With it you still may become sidetracked, but never lost.

Once that you have defined what you want, you can get it by sharing this vision with your team members. Once you have a vision make it known to the people who can make it happen. Make your team a part of your vision.

A Team Meeting for Vision

Schedule a team meeting of at least two hours and no more than four hours in length. A week in advance of this meeting hand out a copy the Team Survey below to each team member and ask them to answer the questions. Ask each team member to write down their ideas and come prepared to share.

Team Survey

1. Regarding our practice of dentistry, what is the promise that we make to our patients?

2. What is the promise we make to staff members?

3. What is the promise that we make to our owner, doctor(s), and stock holders?

Mission Meeting Format

- At your team meeting use an easel pad and markers to record the answers from each person and hang those pages around the room.
- Talk about what you want to experience in your relationship as a team.
- Talk about why those things are important to you and how they make you feel.
- Decide what items are really important to all of you and condense them into a mission statement.
- After the meeting, have someone type a draft of your mission statement. Before your next meeting, provide a copy of the draft to each staff member for their suggestions.
- Polish and complete your mission statement in a follow-up meeting.
- Finally, plan strategies to carry out your mission including a code of conduct or group agreement. See the example on page 48.

If you already have a mission statement, review and update it following the process above. Schedule a time yearly to recreate your personal and team vision together. The world is changing rapidly. You are changing. Your team members are growing. The process of renewal will energize each person. The *process* is essential.

Sample Mission Statement

Promise to Patients

We promise to provide the best, most up-to-date dental care available, in a physically and emotionally safe environment. We promise to be our best at every moment for you with our focus on you and your needs, wants, and desires. We appreciate and gratefully receive the confidence you show by doing business with us, and referring your family and friends. We promise that you will be informed before services are performed, and that you will have the opportunity to choose your treatment and care. We want to work in partnership with you for your best health.

Promise to Employees

We believe that to provide health care we must be healthy ourselves, therefore, we will endeavor to create a healthy, safe, work environment. We promise to encourage your personal and professional growth through continued education and up-to-date training.

We expect you to grow and to contribute at the highest level of your potential. We believe in your ability to be creative, committed, and consistent in your contribution to the success of our practice. We will encourage you to set high standards and goals for yourself, and we promise to acknowledge and celebrate your success.

We promise to share the practice success with you by talking, at least yearly, about your goals and salary expectations. We promise no less than ______ percent of net production to be in salaries. Your rewards will be directly related to our results.

You have the authority to call a meeting with any team member, or all team members, at any time you need help or behavioral changes to support you in reaching your job-related goals.

We want you to feel good, enjoy your work, and have fun every day.

Promise to Owner

We will show up with a conscious choice to be at our best every day. We will contribute 100 percent to the successful growth of the practice. We will be willing to give you, the doctor, feedback to help. We will not withhold our personal convictions because we know they make up the heart of the practice.

We promise to do our best each day to be professional and ethical, and to represent you with integrity. We will respect each other, understanding that each team member offers a special, unique gift to the team. We will be honest with each other. We will work at becoming a great team with the promise of increasing not only our financial rewards, but the profitability of the practice.

Sample Code of Conduct for Team Meetings

- ❑ **Be present and punctual.** Team members will attend all meetings (except for illness or vacations) and be on time. The group will monitor itself to start on time.
- ❑ **Listen and respect.** Team members will promise to let everyone have their say and to show respect for other ideas.
- ❑ **Practice win/win.** Team members will strive to make each team decision be a "winning situation" for all involved.
- ❑ **Be positive.** Team members will adopt a positive attitude toward new ideas, actions, and recommendations.
- ❑ **Stay on target.** Team members will focus their attention and energy on the item being discussed.
- ❑ **Be democratic.** During team meetings, all members are equal and should freely express their opinions regardless of their status (boss/employee) outside the meeting.
- ❑ **Follow through.** Team members will complete assignments when promised and as promised.
- ❑ **Don't be shy.** Team members will ask questions if issues are unclear.

★ **Warning:** Please do not copy the samples and try to install them like a piece of new equipment. The power of the mission and group agreements comes from the *process* of creating them together.

CHAPTER 3: SELF-CHECK

- ❑ I have read Chapter 3 and completed the mirror questions. What behaviors may be incongruent with what I want?

  What can I change?

- ❑ I will create (or renew) the mission of the practice with my team by:

  <u>Action Steps</u> <u>Time Frame/Date</u>

4. BUSINESS MANAGEMENT

"Definiteness of plans: The successful leader must plan his work and work his plan. A leader who moves by guesswork, without practical, definite plans, is comparable to a ship without a rudder. Sooner or later he will land on the rocks."

– *Napoleon Hill,* Think and Grow Rich

In this decade there is peer pressure to save money, invest for the future, and avoid unnecessary interest charges. That is the good news. The bad news is that many professionals have been influenced by the desire to compete for bigger practices, bigger staffs, bigger buildings, and ever growing cash flow demands. Many have measured their success by comparing themselves with others in the profession.

Avoid judging yourself and others. Avoid comparing yourself to another. You are an original. So is everyone else.

The 1990s find us with many choices regarding practice style. Unfortunately, most dentists do not clearly understand the probable consequences of each choice.

Look back at the previous chapters to the values you have defined. What does success mean to you? What constitutes quality of life for you? Let's match your values to what you want regarding your money and your time. Forget the "shoulds." Consider what is right for you.

Let the following examples stimulate your thinking. They describe two styles of fee-for-services dentistry and the probable consequences of each style. Do not allow either example to limit your creativity. There are unlimited combinations. You have the right to choose what you want.

"There are no limits to the mind except those we acknowledge." –Napoleon Hill

---

High Volume Focus

You may opt for the most opulent office and the newest equipment with leading-edge technology. The space and design probably require a large staff, which may include employee doctors or future partnership associates. Some elements of this are:

- higher and higher production/collection goals,
- high new patient goals requiring internal and external marketing,
- high patient retention goals,
- growing patient base with a high volume patient flow, and
- production goal priority leading to increasing accounts receivable.

Predictable Consequences

The large patient base requires multiple hygienists, assistants, and administrative staff. Management and communication needs are high. The size of the organization may lead to bureaucratic hierarchy, unless leadership establishes self-directed teams. These teams become a major focus for in-office human resource training and development.

Unless staff are developed as a primary resource to profitability, payroll overhead including payroll expense and benefits will probably average 30 to 35 percent of gross production. Building and equipment leases may be as high as 10 percent. Variables, 20 to 25 percent. Sterilization and OSHA requirements may cost another 3 percent. Overhead in this style of practice may easily be 65 to 85 percent of gross production.

Intrinsic Motivators

- looking good
- prestige
- service
- professional esteem
- recognition
- newest technology

High Profit Focus

At the other end of the scale is the practice with focus on profitability. This requires a small, effective staff and leased modern space with a conservative focus on updating technical services. There is probably one doctor, one hygienist, one assistant, and one business office person.

Crown and bridge work is 50 to 100 percent of dentist services. Hygiene carefully utilizes a periodontal program that tracks and retains referrals made to a periodontist. Payroll does not exceed 20 percent. High quality service is emphasized. Financing is provided through outside resources. This focus on the quality of patient experience requires highly developed communication and behavioral skills in the doctor and all team members.

Predictable Consequences

The dentist is rewarded with before tax profits of 40 percent or more. Staff members can earn high salaries with incentive paid on a payroll that is 20 percent of production. Services are targeted to those who value the quality of the experience and excellence. Some people will not qualify economically to be patients.

The leader must be committed to keep their part of the bargain with shared profit as the extrinsic motivator.

Staff overhead will not exceed 20 percent; lab, 15 percent; other variables, 10 percent (lower cost due to fewer patients); building and equipment 5 to 8 percent. Leftover work will be handled by core team members or delegated to a low-cost temporary service. Dental supply representatives will manage inventory and new materials. There is a daily and hourly focus by doctor and staff to keep commitments with high accountability for results.

Intrinsic Motivators

- profit
- time off
- flexibility

In Between

Your choice of practice style may be somewhere in between these two options.

In either direction, if you know where you are going, you have a much better chance of getting there. As the business owner, your position requires that you plan where you are going.

Irresponsible ownership fails to plan for profit. Profit is basic to business success.

HOW MUCH IS ENOUGH?

"Success is results turning out as hoped for."

This hoped-for success is a feeling. No amount of money equals happiness. Like happiness, the *feeling* of success, and the satisfaction it brings, is what we strive for. Cash is not a feeling.

Take Charge

❶ Define your goals in writing and evaluate year-to-date monthly statistics. Refer back to your vision to be sure that your plan for profit is congruent with your values.

If you have never done this kind of planning before, consider meeting with a competent and trustworthy financial planner to define your long-term needs. This planning should be done as a family. Include your spouse in creating the vision which will help secure your success.

❷ Take charge of your own financial future. Accountants and financial advisors will do only what you direct them to do. Direct them to help you plan for your vision. Ask them to educate you about investments and long-term results. How will you feel when you can see financial security in your future?

Begin at the Bottom Line

How much do you need before taxes?

❶ Once you know what your bottom line target is, utilize a monthly and year-to-date overhead analysis to compare the ratios. With consistent allocation of expenses, you can monitor your results. You also can do a very accurate cash flow projection. Remember that some costs may vary from month to month because you pay some items yearly and quarterly. When you have calculated your target profit you can clearly define your overhead goals.

❷ Compare your expenses to the optimum ratios as a starting point. Then relate them to your values and keep your own track record. If you compare yourself to yourself as your practice grows, you will have a more realistic measure of results.

Remember that *balance* is required of authentic leaders. You have defined desired results through deductive reasoning. Now, plan strategies that will be congruent with the needs, beliefs, and values of the human beings you work with and serve.

❸ Look back at your values in regard to time. What do you want to experience more of? Plan your time to allow for a balance of work and play, giving and receiving, self-care and group experience.

Stretch your expectations beyond material rewards to measurements of good accomplished:

- satisfaction with self,
- satisfaction with the experiences of the day,
- service to patients in creating trust and partnership for health, and
- honest feedback with team members, ideas shared, enthusiasm and energy.

❹ When you have decided how many days you will do dentistry in a year, calculate your daily production goals. Reserve at least one day per month for team interaction and planning.

If we focus only on money, there will never be enough. If we focus on service and quality, the money will follow.

To whom much is given, much is required. Dentists have been given much. You have the opportunity to represent our noble profession with healing relationships, honest interactions, and a contribution to society equal to your own vision and passion.

Enlightened leaders want to leave the world a little better than it was when they came.

STAFF CONTRIBUTION TO SUCCESS

Give what you want to get. After planning your own long-term financial outcome, you have the opportunity to coach your employees in taking charge of their financial future. A small amount invested consistently in an IRA or pension plan over a number of years will result in financial security for them as well.

Too many times I have seen pension plans contrived for the wrong reasons. Staff members are told of this great benefit, but they never see any financial reports. They are included in profit sharing, but there never has been any profit!

Like you, your team members are motivated by feeling successful, appreciated, and in control of their own destiny and financial future.

What loyalty might you experience if you care enough about your employees to coach them for their own personal success?

It is "penny wise and pound foolish" to contain costs in payroll at the expense of rewarding results. We face a labor shortage in qualified and skilled dental personnel. Every time you have to hire a new employee, your business experiences a loss. According to the American Association of Personnel Consultants, the cost of replacing an employee is equivalent to that person's yearly salary. It is a huge cost that effects *your* bottom line.

So, when you get together with your peers at the local society meeting and hygienist salary comparisons start, excuse yourself. Your peer does not have the power to leverage your profit. Your staff person does. If your numbers are improving it is due to committed, loyal team members working with you to make it happen. If your numbers are not improving, discuss the goals with your team member who can affect change, not with your peers who can't.

Many dentists are reluctant to talk to their team about overhead and net profit because they are afraid staff members will be judgmental about the dentist's earnings. Experience has shown that staff members who know only the production and collection numbers greatly overestimate the net profit. When you define the expectation of production, collection, and overhead goals, you allow your team to contribute to the whole picture.

THE WINNERS CIRCLE

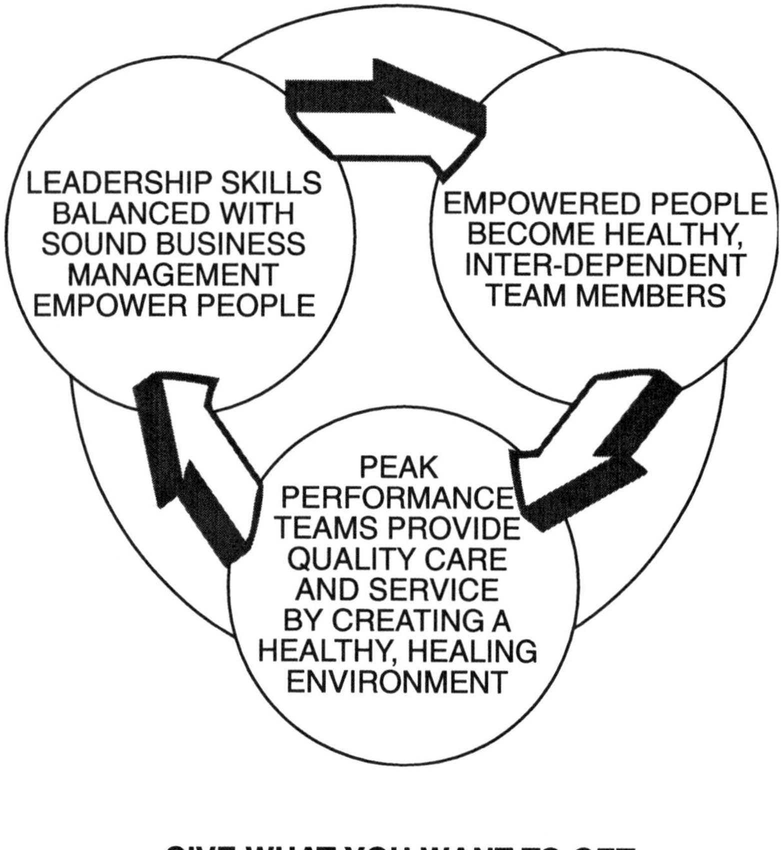

GIVE WHAT YOU WANT TO GET

"Male or female, the effective leader wins commitment by setting an example of excellence: being ethical, open, empowering, and inspiring."
– *Naisbitt and Aburdene,* Megatrends 2000

The most straightforward way to earn loyalty is through honest, ethical management.

People want to know what is going on in their company. The leader who expects results must first give people free access to information.

"An employee without the information cannot take responsibility. With information, he cannot avoid taking it." – Jan Carlzon quoted in Megatrends 2000

Professional team members who are committed to the vision of serving people are intelligent enough to understand practice overhead and to contribute to solving problems. If your intention is to be clear with the staff about goals and statistical objectives, then you must educate staff members about the business requirements of the practice.

Clear as Mud

I remember the day I facilitated a conversation between a wonderful hygienist and her employer. She was convinced that she was being underpaid. Her friends had told her that a certain percentage of her production was a reasonable salary. They also made hourly wage comparisons that are common in our industry.

In this conversation with the hygienist, my intentions were: 1) to be honest, 2) to clarify expectations for this particular practice, and 3) to define a match or mismatch in expectations. I explained that unrealistic expectations may threaten the relationship between the hygienist and the dentist. I expressed my genuine concern because she was the best hygienist we had ever had in this practice.

I continued by saying, "It is true that 35 percent of hygiene production is a fair salary in *some* practices, and you *might* find a job for $40 per hour. In the long term, however, that kind of agreement would be unfair and ultimately destructive to *this* practice."

I proceeded to draw a pie chart of overhead for this particular practice. We had been tracking expenses for several years and were able to compare apples with apples. I could show the dentist's intentions to fairly compensate all team members, to offer benefits, and to meet the profitability requirements. ***Clearly defined expectations,*** offered honestly with the intention of allowing the hygienist to choose what she must do, resulted in her agreement to a yearly salary plus benefits.

Management by intimidation is obsolete! Authentic leadership clearly defines what is expected, plays fair (does not change the rules), monitors results accountably, and reports the results to the people who make a difference.

Information is power only when it allows team members to make course corrections. If you wait until the end of the month or the end of the year to provide monitored information, it is useless history.

ADDITIONAL HELPS

Payroll Overhead Analysis

The Payroll Overhead Analysis on page 64 may be helpful when showing staff members how the payroll portion of overhead is allocated between hygiene and other payroll. Use it to test probable results when making salary changes.

With periodontal and preventive care, hygienists can produce three to four times their gross salaries. By including your hygienist in team decisions and by demonstrating the overhead requirements, you can enroll them in pro-active planning for hygiene department profit.

Hygienists can contribute to practice success in many ways:

- production
- patient rapport and clarifying values
- selling quality care
- enrolling patients in health partnership

Every effort must be made to honor each team member's role. The team must model partnership in patient care. A straight ratio of production pay is not recommended for hygienists because this arrangement threatens the partnership – it may put a limit on how much other staff members can earn. A bonus for production beyond four times gross is more appropriate. Bonus incentives are discussed further in Chapter 6.

Statistics

Statistics should be monitored monthly and reported to the entire team. Page 65 provides a chart for monitoring statistical data. For example:

- Crown and bridge should be 35 percent or more of gross production.
- Fees collected at time of service (ATS) should be at least 30 percent of gross production.
- Hygiene daily averages can be tracked to assure balance in production departments.

Individual team members are made accountable for their particular areas. Hygienists source hygiene production goals; your scheduling specialist sources ATS and production; your credit manager can source collections and accounts receivable. The dentist is the source of crown and bridge through effective communication of benefits and thorough diagnosis. Chairside assistants source getting the job done on time, with comfort and care.

New Patient Monitor

The New Patient Monitor on the opposite page can help track amounts of diagnosis and accepted diagnosis treatment. About 80 percent of new patients should come by referral from your satisfied patients. Emergency patients are not counted as new patients until they have an initial complete exam or co-diagnosis.

It is impossible for your scheduling specialist to book a $2,000 day without accepted treatment coming from the operatory. Since new patients are a primary source of diagnosed treatment, this monitor provides indicators of communication skills in your team. At least 60 percent of diagnosed treatment should be accepted. Treatment is accepted when financial arrangements are complete and treatment is scheduled.

Monitor treatment presented and accepted. Use this information to encourage every team member to continually develop more effective listening skills.

NEW PATIENT MONITOR

Month________________, 199___

Name	Emer. Date	Exam Date	$ Case Pres.	$ Accept Complete	$ Accept Phase	Financ. Code	Referral Source	Type of Acknw.	Date

PAYROLL OVERHEAD ANALYSIS

	Doctor Production	Hygiene Production	Total Production	Hygiene Salary Fixed	Hygiene % Fixed	Payroll Others	Hygiene Variable	Hygiene % Variable	% Payroll Fixed	% Payroll Variable	% Lab	Total Lab/Payroll
1	$28,080	9,600	37,680	3,200	9%	7,627	3,840	11%	29%	32%	10%	29-39%
2	$32,000	9,600	41,600	3.200	8%	7,627	3,840	10%	26%	28%	12%	28-40%
3	$28,080	12,000	40,080	3,200	8%	7,627	4,800	12%	27%	31%	10%	37-41%
4	$32,000	12,000	44,000	3,200	7%	7,627	4,800	11%	25%	28%	12%	37-40%
5	$45,000	9,600	54,600	3,200	6%	7,627	3,840	7%	20%	21%	15%	35-36%
6	$45,000	12,000	57,000	3,200	6%	6,240	4,800	8%	17%	19%	15%	32-34%
7	____	____	____	____	____	____	____	____	____	____	____	____
8	____	____	____	____	____	____	____	____	____	____	____	____
9	____	____	____	____	____	____	____	____	____	____	____	____

These rows are for your own calculations.

CALCULATIONS

- Other salaries are calculated for two persons, $12.00 per hour x 80 hours per week x 52 weeks which equals $49,920.00 divided by 12 equals $4,160.00.
- Add two persons, $10.00 per hour x 80 hours per week x 52 weeks equals $41,600 divided by 12 equals $3,467.00, for a total of $7627.00.
- Hygiene fixed calculated at $25.00 per hour x 8 hours a day x 16 days a month.
- Hygiene variable calculated at 40 percent of hygiene production.
- Reduced other payroll (Line 6) calculated with three persons at $12.00 per hour.

STATISTICAL DATA YEAR 19

Number of charts active 24 - 36 months: _____ divided by 12 = ____ recall per month = _____ days = _____

Month	Accts. Rec.	Production	% CB	Collection	% ATS	Hyg. Days	Hyg. Prod.	Hyg. Avg.	# NP	DR. Day	Avg. Prod.	Avg. Collect.

CHAPTER 4: SELF-CHECK

- ❑ I have read Chapter 4 and learned that:

- ❑ I have completed a personal budget and have set goals congruent with my values and my vision.

  1. Net profit goal $______________
  2. Gross production goal $______________
  3. Hygiene daily production goal $______________
  4. x hygiene days =
     hygiene gross production goal $______________
  5. Practice gross production goal $______________
     minus hygiene production goal -$______________
     equals Doctor gross production goal $______________
  6. I will work ______ days this year
  7. Doctor daily production goal $______________

- ❑ I have a monthly profit and loss statement to work from.

- ❑ Beyond monitoring goals, I value:

  I will keep focus on these intrinsic benefits by:

5. THE SCIENCE OF MANAGING A DENTAL TEAM

"By employing only the hands of workers and not their heads and hearts, organizations lose precious return on their investment in people."

– *James M. Kouzes and Barry Z. Posner,* The Leadership Challenge

The science of managing a highly effective team requires a systematic approach to employee development.

Management principles are made up of four specific stages: planning, organizing, implementing, and evaluating.

As the dentist, you oversee patient management by:

❶ planning treatment,
❷ organizing the sequence of treatment,
❸ implementing each phase by scheduling the work, and
❹ evaluating the patient's condition through the framework of regular preventive maintenance.

These four steps form a cycle of scheduled interaction by the health care team with the patient. This is an ongoing process. Successful results are seen when the patient and the health care team become partners to achieve optimum health benefits.

Coaching a dental team effectively requires the same four steps which serve as the framework for individual and team development. It is an ongoing process. Successful results are seen when the individuals become inter-dependent partners in the business.

Functioning as a manager rather than a leader, the dentist often tries to do all the planning, organization, and implementation, when much of the work might be handled more effectively by specialists on the team. In a genuine effort to be a responsible business person, the dentist often fails to distinguish the difference between *managing projects* and *developing the people to manage those projects.* With so many projects and so little time, personnel development needs may be ignored by the leader. The result of ignoring the personal development of each individual is office uproar.

OFFICE UPROAR

"Office uproar" is a syndrome that erodes your office's effectiveness. It is quite common and very costly to a practice. Unchecked, this disease can debilitate. Check your practice wellness level by identifying any of the symptoms described below. Then, we'll cover the treatment and cure.

Are your employees in an uproar, saying such things as, "It has been a year since I started here, and I was supposed to have a 90 day evaluation... I'm afraid to ask for it, because I'm afraid there'll be bad news. Maybe I did something wrong. Maybe the doctor doesn't like me!" As assumptions and fear build to catastrophic conclusions, uproar begins to damage the workplace.

When the frustrations of several employees are combined, tension increases. Women working together naturally talk to each other. Their relationships and conversations are important to help them feel connected and supported. Yet, this basic need for belonging, expressing frustrations, and sharing fears can begin to feed on itself.

When a group culture is full of resentment and blame, it becomes toxic. As the office grapevine becomes hyperactive, reasons for the bad feelings are needed, so reasons are created. When sub-groups form, attitudes become increasingly adversarial.

Uproar advances. In this toxic environment people feel at risk. There is sure to be:

- high staff absenteeism,
- stress related illness,
- mediocre performance,
- low energy levels,
- frowns and impatient gestures,
- compromised patient care,
- resentment,
- resistance,
- reduced profitability,
- job dissatisfaction, and
- staff turnover.

UPROAR AND DENIAL

With uproar in full swing, the doctor is in a big dilemma. The employees have no idea what he is feeling because *he doesn't talk about it.* They assume that he just doesn't care, when in fact he is more threatened by this situation than anyone else. He sees what is going on, and has no idea how to fix it. Will it, perhaps, just go away? *Please.*

As the ignoring or denial continues, uproar becomes the norm. The office culture is quite toxic and everyone "just lives with it."

Without a clue about what to do, the doctor can be seen tiptoeing about, ignoring the issue until somebody quits. At that point he says, "Oh well, she wasn't any good anyway. We'll get someone really good this time."

Then, the new person is hired. "This should fix it!" exclaims the doctor. This is called "ostrich management."

The following have been identified as areas of high anxiety for dentists in denial about the uproar level in their practice. Here are the top ten issues that doctors want to ignore:

- performance feedback,
- salary expectations,
- time management for planning,
- celebrations (anniversaries - birthdays - special events),
- gestures of appreciation,
- suggestions and new ideas,
- gossip/overactive grapevine,
- office decor,
- timely decisions, and
- acknowledgment of accomplishments.

Uncomfortable or not, these areas of practice management must be addressed. The good news is that dental office teams are usually small. Unlike corporate or government bureaucracies that continue to patch over such damage, we can change and make repairs that improve the situation without an act of Congress.

Such a solution begins when we give up delusion and confusion and recognize what is going on.

If your office has experienced some of the symptoms just described, *it's not your fault.* It happens constantly in dental offices. The difference, now, is that it is no longer necessary to endure uproar symptoms. You can put an end to Office Uproar Syndrome by using the following prescription.

℞ TREATMENT PLAN FOR PREVENTIVE LEADERSHIP

The benefits of applying the science of managing include more than preventing office uproar. Consider the positive impact of a healthy working environment. As your first line of clients, employees must "buy into" the value of your service. They must believe in the doctor. They must trust the organization.

Such employees can enroll the confidence, appreciation, and loyalty of your patients. They do this not from scripts they have learned, but from authentic expressions of who they are.

The treatment plan for preventive leadership is to apply the four management principles discussed at the beginning of this chapter *to developing your team.*

❶ **Plan** your team's vision, mission, results, and benefits focusing on individual and team development.

❷ **Organize** priorities for the development of people.

- Provide clear expectations.
- Plan for continuing education through training and lifelong learning.
- Inspire and enroll commitment in team meetings.
- Demonstrate leadership by making decisions that only the employer can make.

❸ **Implement** scheduled coaching activities to identify and implement priorities.

❹ **Evaluate** success based on whether results turn out as planned.

For you to accomplish these steps, your employees must feel valuable. If you could give them the same kind of care and attention you give your patients, you would see a wonderful change taking place.

Look at one of your patient records. If you have a reasonable standard of care, you will have a well-organized file for each patient. You can easily track diagnosis, preventive care, existing condition, and recommended action. *Do this with your employee personnel files.*

Charting Professional Development

In addition to a file cabinet labeled "Personnel," with an outdated employee application and resumé on each staff member, create an active document that gets used, not musty.

If you design, implement, and maintain such a document for each staff member, it becomes a tool to help them develop their full potential. This will benefit both the practice and the staff member.

Called a **Personal Development Journal**, it becomes a vehicle for moving toward greater partnership between the coach/leader (you) and the team member/employee. A Personal Development Journal is for use by employees as they learn and develop new skills.

The Personal Development Journal is an involvement tool to help keep team members in the driver's seat of their career path. It is about their responsibility and commitment, two elements you want to introduce from the start.

Create a Personal Development Journal for each employee and keep them in a confidential location in the office.

To assemble Personal Development Journals for your team, you will need:

❑ a three-ring binder (1/2 inch) for every employee and

❑ the following sections with dividers:

1. Personal Development Schedule *(Example form follows.)*
2. Job Description and Performance Standards *(See Chapter 7, Step 1.)*
3. Mission/Purpose *(Developed in Chapter 3.)*
4. Training *(Refer to Chapter 7, Step 5. Include training plans and training debriefing notes here, as well as plans for continuing education.)*

5. Personnel Policies and Benefits *(Include a copy of office personnel policies and employee benefits.)*
7. Goals and Feedback *(Record goals and feedback conference notes as discussed in Chapter 7, Step 6.)*
8. Achievements and Acknowledgment *(Place copies of acknowledgment letters and achievements, Chapter 7, Step 8.)*

EMPLOYEE PERSONAL DEVELOPMENT SCHEDULE

Use appropriate elements from the following form to create a page for the Personal Development section of each team member's journal.

Date: ______________________ through ________________
Name: ______________________ Home Phone: ____________
Birthday: ____________________ Employment Date: ________
Probation Period Ends: ________ Emp. Anniversary: ________
Designated Training Partner: ______________________________

Evaluation Date: _____________
Salary Hr:________ Mo:________ Yr:________
Insurance Benefits Hr:________ Mo:________ Yr:________
Dental Benefits Hr:________ Mo:________ Yr:________
Other Benefits: ____

Evaluation Date: _____________
Salary Hr:________ Mo:________ Yr:________
Insurance Benefits Hr:________ Mo:________ Yr:________
Dental Benefits Hr:________ Mo:________ Yr:________
Other Benefits: ____

Goals specified for merit salary evaluation: (may be attached)

____

Next scheduled salary evaluation : ___________________________
Next scheduled performance feedback conference: _____________

1. Personal Development Journals for New Employees

As you introduce a new employee to the Personal Development Journal concept, tell them how you are committed to having the best people on the planet working with you. Make time to meet regularly with the new team member and find out how they are doing. You will want these meetings to be frequent at first until you believe they are catching on and fitting in.

From the start, assign a training partner to your new staff member. Let the new member know that the partner will work with them to help them succeed. In two weeks, schedule a time to debrief with the partner and the new employee. Ask the employee to bring their Personal Development Journal for updating.

2. Personal Development Journals for Current Employees

Current employees will also need to have their own Personal Development Journals when this system is implemented. To introduce this change in office procedure, tell why you are doing it. Explain why you believe it is important and explain the benefits to them of having the whole office using Personal Development Journals for career development.

You could begin by telling them that you wish you had kept records of all that they have accomplished for the practice and that they have achieved for themselves in the time they have been with you.

Explain that you are creating a Personal Development Journal for each member of the team so that you can keep track of their ideas and so that you can support them in reaching their individual goals. It also gives them a way to tell you what they want and to make sure that you know about the things they are proud of mastering in their work. It serves as a format for coming to agreement about the results you both want to see and a forum to acknowledge the results that have been achieved.

As you do with new employees, schedule individual appointments to talk about their Personal Development Journal. Introduce the journal as an avenue for professional growth. Encourage all members to assume greater responsibility for the success of the whole practice by assuming it for themselves.

Schedule for Coaching

To begin your process of leadership, become aware of each member's contribution and development. This includes identifying and remembering their anniversary date of employment with a special acknowledgment. Actions such as this express caring and attention that enhance their commitment and loyalty back toward you.

1. One time each year do a salary evaluation conference with each employee.

The purpose of this conference is to acknowledge the employee for results and accomplishments. Use a letter of thanks to put the pay raise in writing and to clarify the calculation in hourly, monthly, and yearly salary plus benefits. (See Chapter 7, Step 8.) This letter also confirms when the next salary adjustment will be considered. It helps to separate the salary evaluation from other quarterly performance conferences.

Review personnel policies and rules with your staff member if it has been over a year. Clarify expectations regarding vacation time, responsibility for temporary replacements, effect on bonus plans, and practice profit. Plan for a win/win agreement. Openly discuss employees' personal goals for earnings, continuing education, and professional advancement. Ask what this person values and what motivates them. (See Chapter 6 for a discussion on motivation.)

2. Two or three times a year, schedule a performance feedback conference with each employee. Use these conversations to review goals and compare behavior to desired results. The purpose of these meetings is to require you and your team member to focus collaboratively on performance goals and growth. Results will be increased energy and commitment.

3. Schedule feedback often to support behavioral changes required to accomplish mutual goals. These may require daily, weekly, monthly, or quarterly reports. Include entries on scheduled dates for feedback in the employee's Personal Development Journal.

When you schedule evaluation appointments for new behavior, be sure to allocate enough time. Most projects should have a 90-day evaluation, with feedback and corrective action at 30-day intervals. Your leadership style should evolve from being directive at the beginning of a project to delegating as the employee's competence and your trust grow.

Remember to focus on the desired results. Collaborative evaluation with your team will put you all on the same side.

The Leader's Self-Management Guide

Now that uproar is addressed for employees, how about you? Symptoms of doctors in uproar include:

- crisis management,
- uncertainty leading to procrastination,
- reacting to situations,
- feeling out of control,
- critical blaming behavior,
- constant distractions, dilemmas, and delays.

Time Trap

There is a way out of such uproar. Here are some suggestions that have to do with use of your time:

❶ Schedule planning time for you, the leader, just like you schedule diagnosis time for your patients. Use an appointment book (daily planner) to allocate time to prioritize, organize, and implement the actions that will get the results you want.

❷ Begin each day's planning session with the question: What do I want to accomplish today? This week? This month?

❸ Make your "To Do List."

❹ Prioritize by asking: Which of these are the most important? Which of these move me toward what I want? Select and rank actions by A, B, or C priority with realistic intentions to accomplish the A-ranked actions within the specified time frame.

❺ Ask yourself: Which of these can I delegate? Which require decisions that only I can make?

❻ Evaluate yesterday's list:

- Check off the completed tasks and give yourself credit for doing what you set out to accomplish.
- Review the incompletes and re-prioritize them. Move the important ones forward to a more realistic time frame.
- If the same incomplete shows up day after day, that may be an indication that you really don't want to do it. So, skip it. When the time is right, it will be back on your list!

The 15-Minute Self Manager

If intentional listening is the most important leadership skill, self-management is the second. That means managing your priorities to accomplish what you want.

"I know what to do, I just don't do it!" is a confession heard often in leadership study groups. Stop trying to do it all. Make one small commitment instead.

Schedule 15 minutes of "sacred" time for yourself every day. Keep your commitment to yourself.

One unit of action = one unit of self-esteem

Every time we follow through on a plan of action, we feel more competent to manage our priorities. It builds self-esteem. Start with one small action step.

Learn to self-manage by practicing 15 minutes each day.

"The management of self is critical. Without it leaders may do more harm than good. Like incompetent physicians, incompetent managers can make people sick and less vital." –Warren Bennis and Burt Nanus, Leaders: the Strategies for Taking Charge

---

PROTOCOL FOR THE SCIENCE OF MANAGING

It is the job of a leader to create the vision of a work environment that is healthy, and then enroll team support for the big picture. Delegate the authority to do the steps. Define accountability. Establish the time frames for completion of each step. Be sure the expectations are clear. Provide the tools to begin the project. Celebrate small steps completed.

By following this organizational sequence, you can design and implement a highly effective team approach to your practice.

❶ Create a Personal Development Journal for each employee.

❷ Complete a Personal Development Schedule for each employee.

❸ Do your research.

- Calculate the working hours in each employee's year:

  _____ hours per week x 52 weeks = ______ hours per year

  If an employee is not paid for vacation time, revise the formula to the number of actual work days for a year:

  ____hours per day x ____ days per year = ____ hours per year

- Calculate benefits in the same way.
- Establish the employee's yearly salary. Break it down into monthly and hourly amounts as a point of reference. Be able to show your employee how you have calculated their salary. Avoid misunderstandings.

> **WARNING:** This is a time that staff members feel manipulated. Take the time to explain it clearly and show them the calculations so they understand it. Ask if they have questions.

❹ Use the Doctor's Clarification of Expectations (page 128) to write your expectations of each individual employee.
❺ Schedule a meeting to clarify expectations with each employee. Explain your intentions. Hand the employee your completed Doctor's Clarification of Expectations along with the Team Member's Guide to Clarification of Expectations (page 129). Ask them to consider what you have written and to fill out and return the Team Member's Guide at least two days before your scheduled appointment. Schedule a full hour for the conference during normal work time. This is paid time for the employee.
❻ Before the meeting, review the employee's feedback. Carefully plan for your conversation. Be clear about what you will do.

> **WARNING:** This is the time that the doctor can feel intimidated. These kind of evaluations usually involve a salary evaluation. Decide in advance if a salary adjustment is to be given at this time.
>
> If not, make yourself some notes about the criteria for a salary adjustment. Define a time frame. Plan to be authentic. Be honest.

If you are giving a salary increase, write a short letter that puts this merit increase in writing. Follow the example in Chapter 7, Step 8. THIS IS IMPORTANT. If you can't write a letter of acknowledgment, write a note. Everyone needs and deserves positive feedback.

❼ At the employee feedback conference, use your best listening skills. Be sure that your employee feels heard. This does not mean that you have to make promises or say yes to all requests. Be sure that you have heard the suggestions and requests. Take notes.

❽ Allow enough time to create three goals together. These goals should focus on actions that will energize and excite your staff member *and* achieve the desired results for the big picture.

At this point, when you are well into the cycle of managing for peak performance, there are probably not any big issues or behavioral changes to address.

Place the goals in the Personal Development Journal. Give a copy to the employee, along with form Quarterly Feedback Conference (page 140) to be returned two days ahead of the next feedback conference.

When the goals are written, schedule the next feedback conference. Put it in your daily planner. Have your employee record it in their daily planner. Make a commitment to keep your appointments and your word.

The time between feedback conferences may vary from weeks to months depending on the goals. If the employee needs and requests frequent coaching to change a behavior, the scheduled time may be a five-minute, daily debriefing. If the employee needs directive coaching or training, this can be delegated to a training partner. When people have been with you for a long time, they may only need support.

It is essential to meet at least twice a year. At these conferences, talk, listen, encourage, and support the creation of new ideas and enthusiasm. Keep your word. Use your planner. Never leave an employee conference without scheduling the next time you'll talk.

Keep your word regarding salary increases. Be careful not to create false expectations. Be very clear if your budget may not allow for increases or if the employee is at the ceiling of their salary range. Don't let money get in the way of your trusting relationship. Tell the truth.

Remember to be patient with yourself as you develop coaching skills. Even if you feel unpolished and awkward, you are showing respect and regard for your employee through this attention. It is an important skill that good leaders acquire.

CHAPTER 5: SELF-CHECK

- [ ] After reading this chapter, I can see that I could benefit by letting people manage projects. Some of the projects I would like to delegate are:

  <u>Project</u> <u>Person to delegate to</u>

- [ ] In regard to office uproar, I recognize that I avoid discussing:

  <u>Issues Ignored</u> <u>Action Planned</u>

- [ ] I have reviewed personnel files and understand the benefits of combining record keeping with a forward-looking *Personal Development Journal.* Benefits would be:

- [ ] I will manage myself and my priorities by:

  <u>Action</u> <u>Time Frame/Date</u>

6. THE ART OF COACHING HIGHLY EFFECTIVE TEAMS

"A partnership is successful to the degree that it replaces the traditional 'we versus them' mentality with a new 'we' that allows everyone involved to grow and reach their full potential."

–Frank Sonnenberg, "The Age of Intangibles," Management Review, *January 1994*

The systematic approach to management *science* is balanced with a more intuitive leadership approach in the *art* of coaching. As you will see, this is not a path you walk alone. We are interdependent. We all need each other. Like geese in flight, we each take our turn leading when we are *free to lead.*

Authentic leadership is based on the following teamwork principles:

❶ We are all unfolding, growing human beings with strengths and weaknesses.

❷ Human beings cannot grow in an environment of fear, judgment, or insecurity.

❸ Human beings can identify their own desired results and manage to reach those desired outcomes.

It is highly unlikely that your whole team will see your exact vision in detail. They will, however, understand how to get the results desired from your vision. For the whole team to succeed in achieving the vision, it must be broken down like the pieces of a puzzle, into pieces they can grasp and work with.

Specialists (team members) create their own results. Leaders fit the results together to form the big picture.

Leaders empower and enable their specialists by:
❶ providing a vision of the big picture,
❷ creating an environment in which people can grow,
❸ providing all of the information and resources necessary for specialists to achieve their results,
❹ delegating authority to their specialists to take charge and achieve results,
❺ being available and accountable to hear feedback and give support for continued action, and
❻ letting go.

QUALIFICATIONS OF A COACH

To be effective as a coach you must believe in your team. You must recognize the benefits of diversity and the unique strengths of each of your players. Your ability to focus on the success of each individual keeps them playing their best.

As the coach you have tremendous power. With a word or a gesture you can encourage or destroy. Your greatest success strategy is to be consistent with your vision. With the intention to have everyone be the best they can be, you expand your power by giving it away.

Intention is the basis of communication. If your true intention is to have each team member win, that will come through loud and clear. If there is the slightest doubt in your mind that a team member can succeed, that will be clear as well.

As you coach individual team members you must be very clear with yourself about the long-term results you desire. Your team members will be inspired by your vision of future success, and will be willing to stretch for the results you expect.

Coaching is associated with competitive sports where there is a winner and a loser. Until recently, competitive sports have been dominated by men, played by men, coached by men, and reflective of their traditional experience.

> **WARNING:** The typical dental practice is made up predominantly of female team members. They will resist coaching offered in a male sports model manner.

Little girls grow up playing in small collaborative, leaderless groups. Consequently, as women, win-win is their preference and hierarchy is generally uncomfortable. Successful women's coaches know this.

"Lean and mean fighting machine" is not a female motivational motto! A coach who yells, intimidates, barks orders, and runs a militaristic chain-of-command with "no back-talk" won't be free to lead a female staff because the women won't follow.

Men have a good deal of practice with such coaching because of their experience in sports, the military, and, for some, *dental school.* Most women have had much less experience and very little understanding or acceptance of this kind of coaching.

Historically, in the line of fire or on a dangerous hunt, men learned to follow the leader without question. Women did not have to learn that. The skills of collaboration, cooperation, and group decision-making that historically assured women's survival are also the qualities that can be used to create your successful team. The coaching described in this chapter has a natural fit with the cultural female mode of operation. Women will understand it intrinsically.

CHOOSING THE APPROPRIATE COACHING STRATEGY

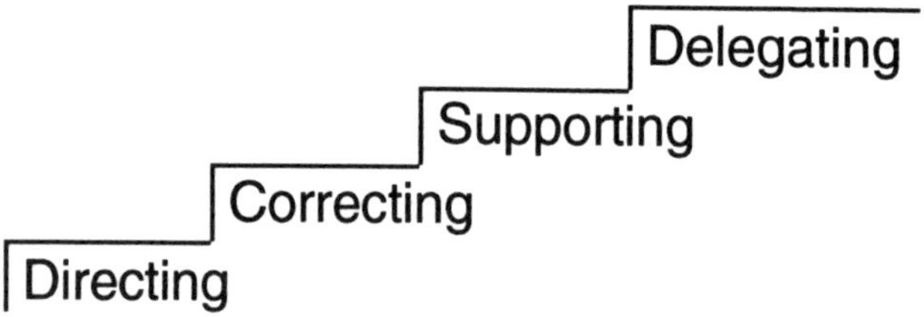

Directive Coaching

Once in a while all coaches encounter a player who is in the wrong game. You may experience it as a sense of uncertainty about whether a staff member will work out. Whatever form this doubt takes, when it strikes, step aside for a moment. Could your self-fulfilling prophecy be adding to their problems? To avoid doing this, let the player prove that they can do the job before you give up on them. This means giving them unconditional support during their learning curve. Clear expectations of results and careful directive coaching is required during this time. *Allow an employee to succeed.*

As the coach, it is important for you to be realistic about the training needs of a new employee. At the entry level it is important for senior managing team members to be directive and tough on trainee performance standards. Most dental teams reverse the order of coaching priorities by trying to make the new team member "feel comfortable and at home" first. There is plenty of time to be supportive after the trainee masters the fundamentals of the job. Set high standards up front!

With directive strategy tied to daily feedback, you soon will be able to define the cause of failure. If consistent coaching for improvement and training is not showing satisfactory results, you may want to terminate the relationship. Before you do this, however, give your new employee a chance to succeed with clear expectations, good training, and consistent coaching.

Corrective Coaching

Here are some examples of effective corrective coaching:

Situation: The employee has been in the practice for over a year. She knows her job, but isn't doing it. She shows up late. Her attitude lacks enthusiasm.

Coaching Action: Schedule a time to meet with her. If confrontation makes you nervous, write notes ahead of time on the items you want to address. Develop rapport by first telling her what you appreciate. Then move into explaining the behaviors that must change. Tell the truth. Use your best listening skills to hear what is *really* going on. Make it a dialog. Define action steps to support her in changing the undesired behaviors. Set a date to debrief her progress and write the date in your daily planner. Keep the notes of your coaching meeting in her Personal Development Journal.

Continued Action: As the employee performance improves, acknowledge her improved behavior and establish the next conference time.

If her performance does not improve, talk again. Use your intentional listening skills. Check for clarity. Define your expectations in measurable goals having her write them down. Set a new time frame for improved performance. Define consequences if it does not happen. Again, check for clarity. Do you both understand this expectation and agreement? If you believe so, have her sign the goal sheet and keep the original in her Personal Development Journal.

Situation: Confidential information about another employee is given to you by a helpful staff member. You are now aware of the rumor of inappropriate behavior, with no proof. You are trapped with the "confidentiality request."

Action: When you are asked to keep confidence about another employee, refuse to do so. Ask the reporting person to confront the situation personally with the other employee. If it turns out to be as serious as allegations of fraud or embezzlement, ask the reporting staff person to join you in meeting with the person in question to express your concerns and ask for explanation. Tell the truth. Be clear about your expectations. Make notes of the conversation and the action to be taken and have both team members sign them. Place the notes in the Personal Development Journal.

Situation: If it becomes evident that the above situation is a power struggle between two staff members, it must be resolved. The resulting negative attitudes from such a situation affect everyone on the team and, therefore, your patients. Your office provides health care. This behavior is not healthy.

Action: Do whatever it takes to resolve a power struggle. This may mean asking for coaching from an outside expert, for example, an accountant, business consultant, psychologist, or attorney. Explore, rather than ignore, your options. You may act as facilitator, or call in a competent facilitator from your local chapter of the American Society for Training and Development. There are straightforward human resource development instruments available to guide you. Arbitration, group process, and conflict resolution are important resources. There are specialists available whom you can call for a particular need.

Supporting the Learning Process

When team members are asked what they appreciate about their employers and co-workers in regard to training, they express appreciation for being shown "how to" while being told "why."

Take the time to explain why things are important. A new skill is more completely learned and retained when it is anchored to additional knowledge. Knowing why something is being taught puts it into a larger context. In this way, team members will find it easier to "buy into" a specific way that work should be done.

"Do it because ..." is a much stronger teaching style than, "Just do it." Offering this insight into the reasons behind your procedures and requests provides the trainee with more reasons to do as you've asked them to do. It demonstrates respect for them and enhances their self-esteem.

Communication, training, and listening take time, yet it is time well spent. Make the time to invest in employees and your business will prosper.

"Anyone who stops learning is old, whether at twenty or eight. Anyone who keeps learning stays young. The greatest thing in life is to keep your mind young." –Henry Ford

---

As your professional team members learn new skills, it is important for you, as a coach, to let go. Much like helping a child learn to ride a bicycle, coaches must resist the urge to run faster and faster to stay alongside. Let an employee wobble forward with you nearby, not hanging onto them.

At the moment that you release control, you empower another with the freedom to fully experience learning. This freedom includes permission, at times, for them to spin out of their learning curve. You can be supportive in helping repair damage and in minimizing failure.

The protocol is first to direct, then to trust, to release, and to trust again. Remember to praise and encourage team members. People thrive under such tutelage. This is supportive coaching.

As people learn new skills they pass through the following stages:

Unconscious Incompetence

You don't know what you don't know and so you feel fine about it.

Conscious Incompetence

You know you don't know. Now you are very anxious.

Conscious Competence

After much practice, crashing, and experience you are conscious that you are now competent, and it feels good.

Unconscious Competence

You've done the job for so long, it has become automatic. You are not even aware of how you do it. You just do it.

Effective coaches understand this cycle and are empathetic to the vulnerability experienced during growth and change. Praise success. Inspire with the vision of the results you want. As you become increasingly able to be patient, honest, and trusting, letting go becomes easier and easier. Remind your team that if it's worth doing, it's worth doing badly at first. Invest in their learning, not in their perfection.

Delegating

The operating style of many competent business staff is to take charge and to do it themselves so they can be certain of the outcome. This is more often true of the business manager than the dentist. For the business manager to delegate and still to be accountable for the results can feel risky. For dentists, there is less concern because they usually are accountable only to themselves. As you develop a highly effective, mature team, you will recognize that team members are all accountable to each other.

In the meantime, there is a way to approach delegation with less risk, more accountability, and better results. The first step is to recognize the limiting nature of "doing it all." When one person does it all, they are withholding the opportunity for someone else to grow. *Delegation empowers others.* To secure a win/win outcome, follow the steps of effective delegation and feedback outlined below.

Effective Delegation with Feedback

❶ Delegate to someone whom you are confident is capable of doing the task.

❷ Do necessary training to allow for success. Take one thing at a time.

a. Show them how to do it.
b. Ask them to show you how they do it.
c. Praise success or go back to step a.
d. Allow for repetition. (It takes 21 days to develop a habit.)
e. Use a training partnership debriefing.
f. Praise and build confidence.
g. Let go!

❸ Delegate the task. Be sure that you agree on the desired results. Choose one of the following five steps:

a. Take action - no further contact with me is required.
b. Take action - inform me of results.
c. Look into the problem - inform me what you intend to do.
d. Look into the problem - provide me with alternative actions and make recommendations.
e. Look into the problem - provide me with facts to help make a decision.

❹ Define the feedback loop.

How will we measure the results? When will we measure the results? What date will we review the project? Who will be accountable to report on it? What happens if we need to change our commitment? Do you have the authority to do the project? What are the support resources available to you?

❺ Use your time planner to make an appointment with your staff member for feedback. As the leader, decide if you need to be directive, corrective, or supportive, or if this assignment is as good as done.

❻ When the task is mastered, define monitors or future feedback frequency if necessary.

❼ Move on to something more challenging. *Acknowledge accomplishments, celebrate growth!*

As your leadership skills grow, they will be contagious. You will have a team full of leaders who are capable of taking leadership in the areas of training, delegating, and reporting their progress through the feedback loop. You will have a SuperTeam!

SUPER TEAM

Based on clear expectations, good training, and teamwork, the leader balances the competence of team members with the appropriate coaching strategy.

COACHING GENIUS

You are beginning to learn to coach a highly effective team.

Brian Tracy, internationally known lecturer and writer says that the following characteristics define a "coaching genius:"

❶ Is able to concentrate without distraction on one situation at a time;

❷ Maintains a "wonder" attitude, is open-minded, and looks at all possible options; and

❸ Always uses a systematic method of problem solving.

The first two characteristics are accomplished through self mastery. The third is simple to learn and an essential skill in the art of coaching.

Systematic Problem Solving

When your team members pinpoint a "breakdown or derailment," some kind of action is required. To ignore the issue or to postpone a decision may put your team back in an uproar. The leader or any team member can learn to facilitate this problem-solving process. The following outline uses the acronym START to make it easier to remember.

Buy an easel and flip-chart pad to keep in your office for team meetings. As you write ideas on the easel pad, you can tear off pages and hang them around the room. They serve as a group memory and allow the facilitator to keep the group on task.

Be prepared for a problem-solving session by having the easel, markers, and tape ready. Select a person to facilitate and another to record.

List the letters S, T, A, R, T down the left-hand side of the first page with plenty of space between letters.

S = Situation

The facilitator asks the group to describe the situation at hand in great detail. Write down the words. Solicit and include each person's perspective. Try to feel what they have said. Before concluding this step, ask the group if they are finished, "Is this list complete?"

T = Target

The word "Target" is used here to identify the real change that is being sought by the team. It moves the group from what they don't want (the situation) into what they do want (the target). After the facilitator asks the group to describe the target, the group should take time to imagine together what they want. Under the heading "Target," list the words they say. Conclude by asking the group if this list is complete.

Stop. The facilitator needs to *pause and be quiet.* People think during silence. Getting over discomfort with silence is a learned skill and significant in the art of coaching. Only move on when the target is clear to everyone.

A = Action

❶ Ask the question, "What can we do to achieve (target words)?" This question is the kickoff for a brainstorming session to set forth the action to be taken.

❷ Brainstorm. This is a rapid-fire process where all participants can speak out and anything goes. The recorder writes ideas as quickly as they are said. **Note:** In brainstorming, ideas are offered without comment, critique, judgment, or "yeah, but" remarks from others.

❸ If silence occurs, the facilitator reads the question again.

Brainstorming should result in at least 20 ideas. Often, the first 10 or so ideas are pretty mundane. Then, out of the pressure to come up with more ideas, people start getting silly. This is the breakthrough into the brain's right hemisphere.

❹ The recorder writes down the silly ideas and encourages more new ideas by asking, "what else?"

❺ When the energy winds down ask, "Is the list complete?"

R = Results

Survey the group for a consensus on the better suggestions that the list generated, marking the obviously bright ideas. Select three to five ideas that answer the target question the best.

Note: Consensus means that the group talks about the ideas enough so that there is support from everyone, even if one group member may not be in full agreement with every aspect of the idea, but agrees to support the process fully. A 100-percent alignment by everyone on all items is not necessary.

T = Tracking

Tracking is another word for project management. To do this, create an action plan listing the project under three headings:

- "WHAT" (the action being taken),
- "WHO" (the person responsible), and
- "WHEN" (the time for completion or evaluation).

Post this action plan in the lab. Highlight completed lines. Check for progress at your next staff meeting.

MOTIVATION

Now we come to the age-old question: "How does a leader motivate people?" Answer: They don't, because people motivate themselves. What the leader *can* do is to create an environment that is energizing. What the team can do together is to a create feelings of appreciation, respect, and accomplishment that are helpful in motivating the entire group.

"Achievement and self-development are now the prime motivators for America's peak performer in business. ... People want meaning. We want to know that our work matters." – Charles A. Garfield, "Six Secrets of Peak Performers," Success, *February 1986*

Job Satisfaction

Career Track leadership training uses the following studies to indicate characteristics of job satisfaction.

In the early 1980s Kenneth Covack reported the ranking of job satisfaction by team members from most to least important as follows. Compare the changing trends of the 1990s.

1980	1990
1. Appreciation	1. Fun and challenging work
2. Being in on things	2. Tactful discipline
3. Sympathy for problems	3. Appreciation
4. Job security	4. Good pay
5. Money	5. Security
6. Interesting work	6. Promotion opportunity
7. Promotion opportunity	7. Good working conditions
8. Loyalty from company	8. Feeling in on things
9. Good working conditions	9. Loyalty from company
10. Tactful discipline	10. Help with personal problems

A 1985 University of Michigan survey asked "What do you want most in your inner world?" The results were:

1. Be listened to (value)
2. Praise - acknowledgment
3. Touch (be present)
4. Feedback
5. Privacy respected
6. Boundaries respected

This is what the research shows. What do you think?

Motivation is much more than financial compensation. Motivation of people has to do with *individualized* feedback regarding *their results.*

People love strokes for doing things. "We need to catch people doing things right," says Ken Blanchard, author of *The One-Minute Manager*. Know what team members have done. Wander around and ask specific questions.

In order to lead our patients to a healthful preventive process, we must model health in our organizations and in our relationships.

The following exercises provide a vehicle for you to find out what is important to your team members.

Staff Survey

Ask your staff members to prioritize the following work satisfaction elements from 1 to 10, with 10 being the *least* important. Insight from this will help you reward employees with what they want.

___ Feeling "in" on things
___ Good working conditions
___ Full appreciation of work done
___ Good wages
___ Sympathetic understanding of personal problems
___ Job security
___ Promotion and growth within company
___ Tactful disciplining
___ Interesting work
___ Management loyalty to employees

The "What's In It For Me" Test

"What's in it for me?" This is the primary motivator of performance for staff members, patients, dentists, and growing human beings in general. Find out what people want and give it to them if you can! If you can't, then tell them why not.

How will you know if you don't ask? This is about clarifying expectations. **Ask! Listen! Take notes.** Be respectful of individual initiative. Never try to second guess what people want. As a rule, clairvoyance is unreliable.

Non-money Motivators (Intrinsic)

To identify their intrinsic motivators, ask staff members these questions:

1. What motivates you?
2. What do you perceive as valuable?
3. What do you like most about your job?
   Be sure their job continues to include these things.
4. What do you like least about your job?
   Delegate it away from them or balance it with things they like.
5. What do you want to be doing in the future?
   How can we help?
6. What would you like to learn?
   Provide these opportunities.
7. When do you do your **best** work?
   Schedule their work with this in mind.
8. Who do you enjoy working with the most?
   Plan projects or tasks with this other person.
9. What is most important to you on the job?

For people at the top of the pay scale, motivate with: recognition, time off, challenging assignments, participation in goal setting, and ownership in the job.

Money Motivators (Extrinsic)

When it comes to money motivators, consider these five points.

1. Base compensation on capability and performance, not on age or tenure.
2. Create incentive pay for performance beyond expectations.
3. Link organizational financial success with individual success. Eighty percent of the companies who have profit sharing experience ten percent more profit than those without. Wal-Mart has over 6,000,000 participants in its profit-sharing plan.
4. Link team performance to individual success (team meetings and monitors that focus on contribution).
5. Reward individual performance with direct compensation. Take time to write a personal letter with every salary increase, which ties the reward to performance in a personal fashion.

STAFF SALARIES AND TEAM INCENTIVES

Money is not a primary motivator. It can, however, be a demotivator. Most people enjoy feeling important, needed, and effective. Money becomes a measure of how effective and appreciated they feel. For this reason, I recommend a carefully planned bonus program which directly relates to the effectiveness of the *team*.

When a group of people work together toward a goal and succeed in achieving that goal, it is appropriate that everyone be rewarded and the achievement celebrated.

The bonus plan is not intended to supplement income. It stops being fun when it is expected and budgeted by employees. It is fun when it provides an *unexpected reward.*

Fun is the major benefit of a bonus plan. It is the process of making it happen together, the excitement shared in achieving and exceeding goals. That is the real reward.

All staff members participating in a bonus plan should understand the motive and philosophy involved: The reward is made possible by the *team* effort that allowed the practice to grow.

It is the doctor's choice whether to share the benefits of a growing practice.

Staff members have been known to exclude other staff members from team bonuses by definition of title such as "manager" or "hygienist" in order to increase their own bonus shares. This is counter-productive to the growth of the practice and to the team atmosphere. This kind of manipulation indicates a problem in the team relationship and should be resolved before continuing the bonus plan.

To make your bonus plan more fun and effective, create a graph that is updated daily so that all team members can see the progress and affect the total result. Be creative with this process. Some groups enjoy a celebration for reaching their goals with a dinner out or a trip to Reno or Hawaii. These options can be negotiated by setting aside excess funds for the celebration.

You can have fun while you make your practice grow. As the coach and leader, remember to acknowledge human beings for their participation and contribution to the achievement of your goals.

Some articles in professional journals say that bonuses don't work. They are based on scientific research and they are right! There are also articles which report that a bonus plan is useful. They are right! It's a paradox and it depends on how you choose to motivate your team.

Being free to lead means being *free to decide* for yourself. It means being free to fail and to learn from the experience. It means being free to operate from the values that you have defined and to allow growth to proceed as an ongoing process. If you try to do everything the "experts" tell you, you will go in circles.

Team Bonus Plan

Hygienists earn considerably more per hour than other team members. Yet they are dependent on the teamwork and accountability of each person to achieve their goals. Each team member plays a role in successful case acceptance, production, collections, patient retention, and keeping the schedule productive. The following bonus plan is team-focused rather than individual-focused. It reflects the win/win/win attitude presented throughout this book.

A profit-sharing bonus plan might be better for your team than the outline presented here. Profit sharing is based on an accurate reporting of profitability. In order for it to be perceived as a reward, team members must have access to your financial information and understand their personal impact on it. Individually, they should be mature enough to take ownership in the company. Partners are invested in the profitability of their company. A profit-sharing bonus plan requires sophisticated accounting and profit planning.

The following outline has been used by my clients since 1982 as a successful step in helping their team develop this kind of financial maturity. It is here for you and your team to use only if it matches your desired practice results.

It is generally accepted in the dental profession that staff salaries in a progressive practice should be between 18 and 20 percent of production. To establish a win/win situation for both dentist and staff members, bonuses might be planned for when production and collection averages exceed five times gross salaries.

Monthly bonus sample calculation.

Monthly bonus is calculated using an average of the previous three months' production/collection. In this example gross salaries of $4,000/month x 5 = $20,000 BAM.

Month	Production	Collection	Average	Excess[1]	Bonus[2]
Jan.	$20,000	$19,000	$19,500		
Feb.	$21,000	$19,500	$20,250		
March	$22,000	$23,000	$22,500		
Three Month Average		**$62,250 + 3 =**	**$20,750**	**$750**	**$150**
April	$23,000	$22,000	$22,500		
Average Feb., March, April		**$65,250 + 3 =**	**$21,750**	**$1750**	**$350**
May	$25,000	$24,500	$24,750		
Average March, April, May		**$69,750 + 3 =**	**$23,250**	**$3250**	**$650**
June	$26,000	$25,000	$25,500		
Average April, May, June		**$72,750 + 3 =**	**$24,250**	**$4250**	**$850**

[1]Excess = Average - BAM [2]Bonus to be shared among staff = Excess x 20%

Quarterly bonus sample calculation.

Salaries $4,000/month x 3 months = Quarter gross of $12,000 x 5 = $60,000 BAM

Month	Production	Collection	Average	Excess	Bonus
April	$23,000	$22,000	$22,500		
May	$25,000	$24,500	$24,750		
June	$26,000	$25,000	$25,500		
Total			**$72,750**	**$12,750 x 20% = $2,550**	

Repeat calculations for July, August, September.

GROSS SALARIES x 5 = BAM (*Bare Actual Minimum necessary to keep salaries at 20 percent of production/collection*)

Any time salaries are increased through raises or adding another staff member, BAM is recalculated.

Whenever BAM is exceeded by production *and* collection averages over a three-month period, the doctor agrees to pay 15 to 20 percent of the excess in a bonus to be shared *equally* by all staff members. See the chart at left for sample monthly and quarterly bonus calculations.

Employee bonus calculations.

The bonus share for staff members is usually determined by time worked. If a person works two of four days possible a week, that portion would be half of full time. To calculate part time, take the fraction of days worked multiplied by full-time bonus. Using the first example in the chart, with a shared bonus of $150:

2 full-time employees + 1 half-time employee = 2.5 ÷ $150 bonus =

$60 for full-time bonus and $30 half-time bonus

To double-check: $60 + $60 + $30 = $150

When a plan is established, set the date for a team evaluation. Define how, when, and under what circumstances the bonus agreement may be changed. Be absolutely sure you are committed to share with the team *before* you promise to do so. *Bonus checks given with a frown are worse than no bonus at all.*

Remember what you are trying to accomplish with any incentive plan. It is intended to energize everyone. Its effectiveness should be evaluated at your yearly planning session.

CREATING A HEALTHY WORK CULTURE

Many staff members tell me that they love their work, but the gossip, back-biting, and adversarial conditions in the office make them sick. On the other hand, doctors tell me they won't have staff meetings because they turn into complaint sessions. Remember office uproar?

Motivating employees is important, but ineffective without removing de-motivators from the workplace.

Pay Attention to the "Not So Obvious"

Perhaps you have called in a business consultant. To their eye everything may look good. The numbers may look good. The ratios may check out.

Yet, there is friction within the team. Nobody talks about it. When the consultant asks about the discrepancy between how things look and how they feel (if they are intuitive enough to notice), the client responds, "Oh, we just have some personality differences, but we are very careful not to let them show. Our patients would never know."

NEWS FLASH! If *you* feel tension, *everybody* feels it.

What we are feeling is also converted into self-talk. Self-talk is the internal dialogue we have with ourselves. Those around us may feel our discomfort, but we actually hear about it! We begin to have internal doubt dialogues that sound something like: "He must be mad at me. I wonder what I did wrong. Maybe my job is on the line!" or "She makes me feel guilty."

Such self-talk creates insecurity and defensive behavior within an office as illustrated in the iceberg. On the surface everything seems normal, but the underlying problems may be overwhelming. When the symptoms show up in your practice, you can change them by getting at the root of the problem.

ICEBERG OF OFFICE CULTURE

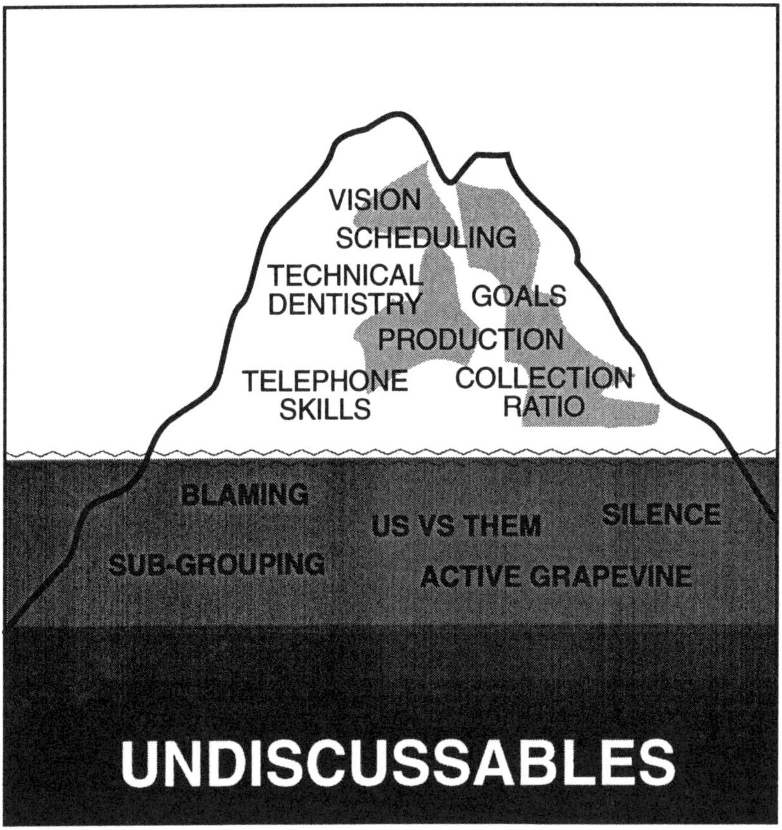

To break this cycle of tension, negative self-talk, and assumptions, we must be willing to acknowledge hidden agendas. Hidden agendas include "undiscussables" such as:

benefits	personal lives	doctor's wife	salaries
job security	patient complaints	gossip	personalities
profit	quality of work	bonus	authority

If this iceberg exists in your office it will help just to admit it. Making time to listen to each team member and follow the systematic approach of the leadership cycle will resolve many concerns by putting the undiscussables on the table. Other issues can be handled in group problem solving or by making group agreements for open communication.

Resolving conflict is an ongoing process of human interaction. Individuals mature through the experience.

CHAPTER 6: SELF-CHECK

❑ After reading Chapter 6, I understand that coaching should be directive when:

supportive when:

❑ I can be more effective in delegating by:

❑ I have reviewed motivators with each employee and have invited their ideas by:

❑ I will help my team learn the steps of systematic problem solving by:

7. THE LEADERSHIP CYCLE

"It is the leader's role to lift followers out of their everyday selves up to a higher level of awareness, motivation, and commitment."

– *Donald T. Phillips,* Lincoln on Leadership

By now you have explored the concepts of leadership and what followers expect. You have identified what you want in your professional life. You have given some thought to identifying your values and bringing your vision to life through self-management. You have discussed your vision with your staff and have clarified your team mission.

You have defined financial security for yourself and your staff members. You have identified your overhead and profit objectives. You have learned diagnostic indicators of office uproar and a prescription for preventive leadership.

You have learned to apply the appropriate coaching strategy and to motivate your team.

Now you are ready to enter into the leadership cycle. This systematic framework plugs the science of management into the art of coaching, bringing life to your leadership.

The leadership cycle is easy:

Step 1. Develop a job description and performance standards with each employee.

Step 2. If you have vacant positions, determine who you want to fill them.

Step 3. Interview and hire the person you want to be on your team.

Step 4. Know what results you expect from each employee and make sure they know them and are committed to achieving them.

Step 5. Provide training so employees will know how to achieve the desired results and why they are important.

Step 6. Set goals with each employee with a plan for achieving them. Schedule feedback conferences to review progress and set new goals.

Step 7. Support your team members individually and as a group.

Step 8. Evaluate individual salaries with each team member and acknowledge their accomplishments.

THE CYCLE OF LEADERSHIP

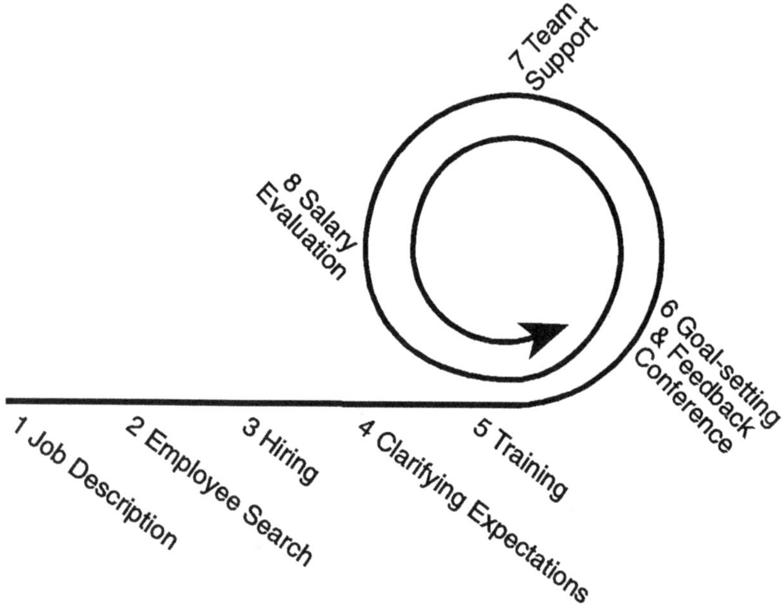

This chapter covers each of these steps in detail with examples to illustrate them. Once steps 1 through 5 are accomplished, you are ready to roll! Use your daily planner to:

- plan quarterly goal setting and feedback conferences,
- note support dates and celebration plans, and
- schedule annual salary evaluations.

At this point you are in the loop. But if you experience a derailment, the last section of this chapter will help you get back on track.

STEP 1. CREATING THE JOB DESCRIPTION

Enlist each employee in the task of creating a job description for their position by asking the following of them:

❶ *If there is not a written description of your job, please make a list of what you do daily, weekly, and monthly. This may take a few weeks to accomplish. Plan time with me (the doctor) and with other team members to get this job done. You may delegate the typing or computer input for this.*

❷ *When you have completed the list of things you do, add a list of* ***performance standards*** *(see examples on the next few pages) that go with the identified tasks of your job. Performance standards will make your special role clear to both new and current team members.*

❸ *Once a year, when the whole team does planning, review your job description and performance standards. Then make any changes and additions.*

❹ *When completed, a copy will be placed in a personnel training manual crediting you as the author.*

❺ *File a copy of your completed or revised job description in your own Personal Development Journal under the "Job Description" section.*

Job descriptions differ for each role in each dental office. These focus on the tasks that each employee performs. Performance standards are more universal and focus on the purpose for each role and on areas of responsibility. Note the examples on the following pages.

Performance Standards: DENTAL ASSISTANT

Purpose: To work cooperatively with the dentist and other team members to assure personalized professional dental care for each patient. In order to accomplish this purpose, you should:

- Utilize the internal paper flow (treatment router and superbill or charge slip) to plan your day.
- Know the treatment to be done for each of your patients so that you can be set up with all instruments, equipment, and supplies necessary.
- Help create a warm, caring environment.
- Be flexible.

By developing the best technical, organizational, and behavioral skills, you can be well rewarded.

Areas of responsibility:

A. Patient Care

- Be aware of expected time of patient arrival. Seat them within 10 minutes of their appointment time.
- Answer questions and calm anxious patients. Talk about the value of dental care with the time you have. Relate on a personal and professional basis with your patients. Never leave the patient alone.
- Be prepared with an updated medical history, treatment plan, radiographs on view box, and set up for procedure.
- Listen to the patient and the dentist. Anticipate needs. Stay one step ahead of what is going on.

- Complete paperwork before you release the patient from the operatory.
- Escort the patient to the business office and transfer them to the receptionist for "fee for today" and "next appointment."
- Define next treatment: tooth number, surface, type of restoration, time in units, and interval on your treatment router.
- Learn charting protocol from your dentist and define accountability for charting.
- Role-play questions so you are able to clarify your dentist's diagnosis in terms of benefits to patients.

B. Sterilization/Asepsis

Know the sterilization procedures set forth by your doctor. These should include proper methods for killing spores and other sanitary procedures. Outline the specifics. Be consistent. Don't take shortcuts! Be able to communicate your care regarding the sterilization techniques used in your office. This will help ease patient concerns about high-risk diseases.

C. OSHA Regulations

Know and comply with all OSHA regulations. Be able to communicate your competence in meeting all health and safety regulations to your patients. Have a written philosophy of patient safety framed and hung in the reception area for your patients to read. Both the signature of the dentist and the patient safety coordinator should be on this announcement. (Give credit to the person who has worked to organize this achievement.)

D. Radiographs

Have current radiology license or certification. Be informed of your dentist's radiology protocol. Take radiographs as directed by the dentist. Be able to answer patients' questions regarding their exposure to radiographs and the need for them.

E. Laboratory Procedures

(Specific to each dentist's protocol.)

F. Inventory Control

(Specific to each dentist's protocol.)

G. Expanded Functions

(Specific to each dentist's protocol.)

Performance Standards: BUSINESS SECRETARY

Purpose: To assure that all business aspects of the practice are functioning in an orderly and proficient manner.

Areas of responsibility:

A. Patient Management

Insure that patients are appropriately seen and treated in a professional and timely manner. You are responsible for:

- Patient contact both telephone and in person, expressing concern and caring.
- Patient records, appointments, information, financial agreements, insurance billing, patient billing, posting, collections, and delinquent accounts.

B. Office Procedures

- Know new patient and emergency new patient protocol. Make good use of the telephone slip with patients. Clarify expectations regarding quality care, payments, and keeping appointments.
- Utilize treatment router to assure completed treatment, to engineer your schedule, and to communicate with the team about financial agreements and short-notice availability.
- Always tell each patient the fees at each appointment for that day. Be sure financial agreement is made, utilizing all

possible options to help the patient receive the recommended treatment.

- Always make the next appointment before the patient leaves.
- Post-treatment charges, adjustments, and payments daily. Generate a computer or posting "day sheet" that provides an audit trail for daily deposits.
- Manage your time to allow for dedicated focus on recall, chart audit, and accounts receivable control (including insurance aging and audit) daily, weekly, and monthly to assure "priority leverage" to reach established objectives.

C. Production

Study the scheduling instructions in your training manual. You are accountable to schedule and meet daily production goals for the dentist and the hygienist. This is accomplished by focus on one day at a time: today, and then tomorrow.

Know the telephone protocol to verify appointment times and to educate patients to be responsible. Know the recall protocol, chart audit protocol, and your accountability in the team effort. Meet with the doctor and other team members to discuss, evaluate, and plan for the production of the practice. Stay attuned and updated so the practice goals can be successfully accomplished.

D. Accounts Receivable Control

Performance standards for accounts receivable control are detailed in your training manual.

The statistics you compile provide you and your team with the "blood pressure" of the practice. You are accountable to report statistics monthly. Most information is readily available from monthly computer reports. Instruction will be provided by your computer trainers. These reports should be made monthly to the dentist, immediately after the month end reports are generated. Review of the aged accounts receivable should be scheduled with the dentist at least monthly.

Know the office credit policy. Know the internal collections protocol. Report your activity regarding accounts receivable weekly.

E. Marketing

Internal marketing ideas are included in your training manual. Know your accountabilities for notes, letters, and projects. All team members can participate in generating internal referrals.

External marketing is specifically defined by your practice. Keeping a new patient monitor regarding referral source and dollar results is very important. You are accountable to be sure this takes place and is reported monthly.

Performance Standards: HYGIENIST

(RDH - State License)

Purpose: To work cooperatively with other team members to create an efficient continuing care (recall) system that communicates with the patients and keeps them active in the practice. In order to accomplish this purpose, you should:

- Utilize your technical and behavioral skill to offer improved and continued dental health.
- Educate and enroll patients in the partnership of regular preventive care and home care.
- Encourage patients to consider the benefits of recommended restorative treatment.
- Listen to your patients. Help them get what they want and need through enhanced communication skills, individual attention, and commitment to quality dental care.

Areas of responsibility:

A. Patient Management

Insure that patients are seen in a professional and timely manner.

You are responsible for:

- Preventive care, periodontal charting, and recording of periodontal diagnosis in diagnosis code and appropriate treatment code.
- Pre-appoint for their next preventive or periodontal treatment. Schedule it in the future book with today's date (in parentheses), defined treatment, units for next visit, and daytime telephone number.
- Coordinate future treatment through computer or manual recall system with the business office. Record the "reason" for specific, individualized follow up on their next visit.

Results of effective patient management:

- 75-85 percent of active patients are current in recall. Every preventive patient knows we welcome new patients.
- Patients understand and value dental health resulting in acceptance of 70-75 percent of all treatment presented.
- 70-75 percent of new patients come from patient or family member referrals.

B. Development of Hygiene Department

- Creatively work with other team members to target growth goals for your department.
- The number of active charts divided by six equals the number of potential recall visits per month. The balance of preventive and periodontal care equals daily production of $600.00 or more.
- Evaluate fees and the value of care based on the time necessary for the condition presented.
- Be aware that your daily goal of $600.00 equals $13.00 per increment (10 minutes) or $80.00 per hour. Create ideas to maximize your time by utilizing other staff members and office space effectively.

- Work cooperatively with the dentist and other hygienists to define a smooth functioning soft tissue management program that allows patients to learn how to help themselves and rewards their progress.
- Cooperate with the business office to identify patients who are available on short notice to assure a productive schedule.
- Keep track of patients' personal values and concerns.

C. Personal Growth and Development

Communicate your ideas and suggestions to the rest of your team. Be committed to the practice and to your patients.

Take continuing education courses that energize you. Ask for what you need, speak your truth. Have a positive attitude. Set challenging goals for yourself. When you achieve them, set new goals. If you don't reach them, ask for help.

Note: *The percentages and dollar amounts used here are examples. Defining your goals is up to you.* The information you get from consultants and seminars is very useful. However, you are *free to choose* what is best for your office and for your mission. There are many right ways to do things.

STEP 2. EMPLOYEE SEARCH

Hiring can be done by anyone. *Hiring for success* requires the entire team. Matching individual strengths to the job description is a very complex challenge. My advice is to use your entire team, encouraging everyone's intuition and input in the process.

To fill a vacancy in your office begin with a team meeting:

❶ Review and update the job description.

❷ Ask for input about the qualities you are looking for. Begin by considering this: "Describe the person we will select as our new (position)."

❸ List traits and strengths on a flip chart for group focus.

Remember that you draw to yourself people who are like you. As you and your team mature, you will draw more mature team players.

Create a Picture of the Person You Want

What you picture is what you'll get. Using an easel to record the qualities you want in the new person, a picture will emerge. When the whole team creates the vision of what they want, it will be very clear when you have a match.

Here is an example of what one team did. In a brainstorming session, desired qualities were listed for the new hygienist. Using that list of qualifications, the team developed an accompanying set of interview questions.

At the completion of this process, the team knew the kind of person they were looking for, and they had a list of questions to use during the interview process.

Examples of Desired Traits and Screening Questions

1. **People person**
   How do you know when you have rapport with a patient?
2. **Focus on patient care**
   Describe a good dental hygienist for me. *(Listen for qualities you want.)*
3. **Clinical skill**
   Ask the applicant to demonstrate technical skill by working for a day. Have them do a prophy on the dentist or a staff member. Check their references.
4. **Stays on schedule**
   How much time do you need for a routine prophy? for a child? for a periodontal maintenance patient?

What does "on time" mean to you? *(Match team expectations.)*
What do you do to stay on time? *(Listen for specific actions to be in charge of self.)*

5. **Professional attitude**
Tell me about your job experiences, both before dental hygiene and since. Of all the jobs you have done, what aspects did you enjoy the most? *(Listen for people related answers.)*
What does "being professional" mean to you? *(Take notes.)*
6. **Caring**
How do you relate to a jumpy, fearful patient? *(Listen for empathy skill.)*
7. **Self-motivated**
Beyond fair compensation, what is important to job satisfaction for you?
8. **Manages time well**
What do you do during a cancellation? *(Listen for willingness to help others.)*
What can you do to assure a productive hygiene schedule? *(Listen for accountability.)*
9. **Team player**
As a dental hygienist, what are you accountable for?
Of those accountabilities, what are the three most important priorities? *(Listen for the ability to take action to make things happen.)*
10. **Good communicator**
Are you willing to take courses and continued education in communication skills?
What do you do to keep communication open with other staff members?
11. **Periodontal training/experience**
Describe your philosophy regarding periodontal care.

Finding the Perfect Match

When you know the qualities you want in your new employee, utilize your network. Tell everyone you know about the open position and describe the person you want to fill it. Suppliers, labs, accountants, consultants, study club peers, associations, and ads are all channels to help you find the perfect match.

Design your ad to match the most important qualities you have defined. Some examples follow.

Sample Ad: Dental Receptionist

We are looking for a very special highly motivated person for our growing family practice. If you:

- Enjoy working with the public
- See yourself as a professional team member
- Are committed to continued learning

We want to talk to you! Please deliver your resumé in person to: __________

Sample Ad: Dental Assistant

We are looking for a very special highly motivated person for our growing family practice. If you:

- Are trained, X-ray Certified Dental Assistant
- With a mission to help people
- See yourself as a professional team member
- Are open to continued learning

We want to talk to you! Please deliver your resumé in person to: __________.

Sample Ad: Dental Hygienist

We are looking for a very special highly motivated person in our growing family practice. If you:

- Are a licensed Dental Hygienist
- With a mission to help people
- See yourself as a team member
- Are committed to professional growth

We want to talk to you! Please deliver your resumé in person to: __________.

Sample Ad: Dentist

We are looking for a technically superior, gentle, and caring practitioner for our solo group. If you:

- Are a licensed Dentist
- With compassion for people
- Are willing to create ideas and solutions
- With a commitment to continued professional and personal growth

We want to talk to you! Please deliver your resumé in person to: __________.

The examples above are offered as suggestions. Your success in drawing the person who matches what you want is enhanced when you have used team input to determine the qualifications desired in a new employee. Use the qualifications you all identify in your ad and design your interview questions around them. Picture the person you want to apply and you'll recognize them when they apply.

Ad spacing and placement are important. The example ads allow you to state your name and address proudly. Post office box ads will not draw as high a quality of applicant.

Initial Screening

When resumés are delivered in person, have your receptionist make notes of her impression of the applicant on the back of each resumé. Instruct the receptionist to tell the applicant that you will be calling selected candidates no later than *(specific date)*. This will relieve you of the obligation to call each applicant.

If telephone screening is necessary, ask the same questions of each applicant so that you will have a similar base for comparison. For example, ask:

- ➤ *Tell me about your previous experience.*
- ➤ *What do you need to have in a job for personal fulfillment?*

Given a positive impression, be prepared to schedule a personal interview with an applicant. At the time of the interview, give them a respectful session, conclude by selling your services (even if you don't hire the person, you may receive patient referrals from this contact), and tell the applicant the date by which you will have selected your finalists. "We will contact the finalists for an interview with staff members no later than *(date)*."

STEP 3. HIRING THE PERFECT MATCH

Interviewing

Use the list of qualities from the team brainstorming session to develop questions to screen applicants for each desired quality. *Use the same set of questions with each applicant.*

Decide who will do the interviews. Be prepared with interview questions, the applicant's resumé and application for employment, and a private place to talk.

First Interview

The following "Interview Evaluation" lists some important characteristics for a quality-oriented, fee-for-service dental practice. Questions or instructions are listed next to each qualification to help you evaluate applicants.

Use a formal procedure for the first interview. By asking the same questions of each candidate, you can rate their responses objectively.

After welcoming the applicant and going over their resumé, let them know that you have a prepared set of questions. Encourage them to relax saying, "There are no right or wrong answers, they simply help us understand what is important to you."

Continue, "It is important for us to find the person that best fits with our team philosophy. I cannot interpret the questions for you, but I can read them over again at your request."

Keep the interview results in a file for each applicant. Review them with other team members. Decide on the finalists. Call to schedule final interviews.

Interview evaluation of ______________________________

For the position of ______________________________

Interviewed by ______________________ **Date** ________

Rate 1 - 10 with 10 being highest.

1. People relation skills

   Question: Is it important that the people you work with like you? How would you like the patients to think of you?

   Rating _____

2. Projects warmth, empathy, spontaneity

   Question: What have you done to help your co-workers enjoy their work? Are you a positive person? On a scale of 1 to 10 with

10 being high, rate yourself as a positive person. (8 or above)

Rating _____

3. Feels good about touching people

   Instruction: During the interview, shake hands or touch the person and note their response.

   Rating _____

4. Has a mission to help people

   Question: Do you have a special mission in life? Tell me about it.

   Rating _____

5. Will be willing to learn and grow in behavioral skills

   Question: Do you have any interest in improving your communication skills? In what areas would you enjoy continued education?

   Rating _____

6. Has required training/experience for the position

   Instruction: Check resumé - references - on job testing

   Rating _____

7. Has desire and ability to learn procedures

   Question: Is it important that people who work together understand all of the office procedures? How much should a good employee know about the technical aspects of the business? *(all that they can to do a better job)*

   Rating _____

8. Has ability to follow outline of instructions

   Instruction: Observe ability to follow interview instructions

   Rating _____

9. Has ability to see long range, future focus

   Question: What do you expect to be doing 10 years from now? *(a definite answer having to do with self growth or improvement)*

   Rating _____

10. Has ability to organize work and priorities

    Question: How do you prepare for a day's work? What makes a really good day for you? How do know when you've had a <u>really</u>

good day? *(completeness, smooth flow, planning, people first in priorities)* Rating _____

11. Has friendly, professional appearance and conduct
 Instruction: Observe Rating _____

Second Interview

Now that you have selected a few finalists, do a reality check to be sure that the mission, standards, policies, and agreements that you have developed as a team are compatible with the candidate's values. Begin the second interview by saying, "You scored very well on the interview questions and with the staff members who have met you. At this point we want to be sure that you want to work with us. Please take a few minutes to read our mission statement and our group agreements. Look over the personnel policy outline and benefits. When you are finished I want to go over them with you and get your feedback."

When the applicant is ready, ask questions like:

- *How would these agreements benefit you?*
- *How do you think your potential might be limited or enhanced by our policies and agreements?*
- *On a scale of 1 to 10 with 10 meaning absolute agreement, and 1 meaning absolute disagreement, indicate your feeling about each agreement.*

Use the same format with all candidates to have a common point of reference.

Nothing affects team relationships so drastically as adding a new team player. When the finalists are selected, preferably three, staff members should visit with them and compare impressions. If your staff members are involved in "picking a winner" they will be committed to making their selection become a winner.

Hired!

When your selection is made, it is important that the new employee read your personnel policy, discuss any questions, and sign the policy. Then place a copy in their Personal Development Journal. The trial period and benefits should be clearly defined to avoid any misunderstanding. Steps to successful integration into the team are outlined in more detail as you follow the leadership cycle.

Good public relations requires gracious handling of candidates not hired. Send a thank you note or letter to express appreciation to those you did not select. For example:

Dear (applicant),

Thank you for the time and consideration you contributed to interview for the position of ________________ .

We have selected another applicant. It was not an easy choice. You have excellent qualifications.

We will keep your resumé on file for 90 days. Best wishes to you in your job search.

Sincerely,
Dr. ______________

STEP 4. CLEAR EXPECTATIONS

Preventive Team Care

When you hire a new person you can prevent misunderstandings by being very clear about your expectations. First, give each new employee their own Personal Development Journal as described in Chapter 5.

Renewing Agreements

To begin coaching current, long-term employees use the outline entitled Doctor's Clarification of Expectations on page 128. It is a leadership tool to be used only once with each employee.

You may wonder why this is necessary with your valued, long-term employees. You may think they know what to do and they do a good job. You talk every day, anyway, solving problems and sharing ideas. This may be so, but this valued friend and associate deserves the best leadership you can offer.

Research examining the relationship between communication and technical performance shows that *lower-performing groups* had been together from *one and a half to five years*. This was accounted for by noting that there are not enough new ideas in such an isolated environment. *The higher-performing groups,* on the other hand, *had significantly more communication with people outside their office.*[1]

Extending these implications beyond the research, we see how some organizations can become myopic and unimaginative. The people themselves are not dull or slow-witted, they simply have become too familiar with their routines and too isolated from outside influences. To infuse fresh ideas into an organization, the leader needs to shake it up periodically.[2]

So, take the Doctor's Clarification of Expectations and read the paragraphs describing its purpose. Do you agree? Each team member also needs to understand its purpose as well.

For help in defining specific areas of accountability and expected results, review the employee's performance standards. Define roles in the framework of *results*. When you tell someone *how* to do something, you demean and limit them. As a leader,

---

[1]Kouzes and Posner, *The Leadership Challenge,* 1987, p. 58.

[2]Kouzes and Posner, p. 59.

you empower people when you allow them to achieve results any way they choose, as long as their method aligns with your values and your mission. Outline your expectations in the form of results that are measurable and place them in a time frame for evaluation.

- Give the team member a copy of the Team Member's Guide (sample on page 129) and ask for thoughtful input.
- Set a date for this conversation with them and outline your expectations in terms of short-term and long-term results.
- Meet during regular work hours in designated management time. Allow plenty of time and don't allow any interruptions. If you put it off or fail to keep your appointment you will create negative results. Reserving personal time for your employees and keeping your commitments enhance their value and self-worth.

Often evaluations have not been done for a long time and salary adjustment criteria have never been defined. If this is the case in your office, examine the salary level along with expectations. Determine next year's salary increases.

You will notice that the Team Member's Guide gives your employee the opportunity to write down how much they are earning (a place to check for clear expectations) and how much they would like to be earning in the future. This is one of the most avoided conversations known to dentistry. Don't be afraid of it. Plan ahead by knowing your practice budget and goals. Ask your employee to hand you the Team Member's Guide two days before your scheduled conference so you can be prepared to respond.

If confrontation makes you nervous, prepare ahead of time and take your notes with you. Be honest about your intention to have open communication and clear expectations. If you feel pressured, say so. You don't have to make any on-the-spot decisions. You can take time to think about it as long as you set the date for the decision. Keep your word. Procrastination will undermine your efforts.

DOCTOR'S CLARIFICATION OF EXPECTATIONS

Job Title: ____________________ Today's Date: _________

Dear ________________________,

The purpose of this conversation is to be sure that you and I have the same picture of the results we desire from this department and this specific job role.

I appreciate the fact that you are the expert working in this area every day. You have the insight to create the methods to achieve the desired results. I want to be clear about my expectations. Then I want to hear your expectations of what you want to accomplish.

Together we will set the goals for your department and define a method to measure the results along with a time frame for achieving them. The results can be related to a predetermined merit raise in salary. I want to support you in reaching your goals and I want you to feel well-rewarded for your creativity in achieving our goals.

While the common measure for pay is based on hours, you are being paid based on your attitude of commitment and the results you are able to effect.

When you encounter obstacles to achieving your goals, I am committed to helping you overcome them. Since most of these obstacles involve behaviors of other team members, myself included, you may respectfully ask for help from the source of any obstacles you experience.

Please bring me your solutions rather than problems. You may schedule management time with me or other team members to effect solutions. I want you to succeed.

Regarding your responsibilities as ________________________ these are the results I expect:

Are these realistic expectations? _________ What did I miss?

TEAM MEMBER'S GUIDE TO CLARIFICATION OF EXPECTATIONS

In order to assist the doctor in the management of results, please fill out the following and return it to the doctor two days before your appointment.

My most important job role is

____

The results I am accountable for in this job role are:

____

Obstacles to achieving the results I desire are:

____

Possible solutions are:

____

Other aspects of my job description in order of priority:

____

The results I am directly accountable for in the jobs listed above are:

____

In order to achieve the results I desire in each area of accountability, I need:

____

My current compensation is:
Yearly __________ Monthly __________ Hourly __________
By _________________ , I would like to earn _________________.
(doctor may fill in date)

I understand that the practice must be profitable in order for the dentist and other team members to be fairly compensated. I can contribute to the profitability of the practice directly by:

____

____

Beyond fair compensation, I value and appreciate:

____

____

Signed: ______________________ Date: ____________________

Defining Boundaries with Team Members

Besides clarifying roles and responsibilities, leaders should clarify expectations about professional behavior and fringe benefits. Written policies and rules help clarify expectations. Policies are one way to avoid misunderstandings about time off, pay, benefits, and potential liability. The term "rules" is defined as clearly stated acceptable and unacceptable behaviors.

Rules become less necessary as leadership skills develop and people become accountable for communicating their dissatisfactions, requests, and feelings. It would be nice to banish all rules in favor of clean communication. Since that is not the case for most offices, however, we must begin with preventive measures.

Written policies regarding benefits help avoid the appearance of favoritism as well as prevent unhealthy competition among employees. Consensus among dental staff members indicates that they don't care as much what the benefits are, as long as they *know what they can count on.*

The benefits you offer are precious to your employees. The rule for the leader is simple: Keep your word. If you must change it, time the change well in advance of the situation in question. While it is impossible to anticipate every misunderstanding, you can prevent most fears and resentment with some simple preventive management.

Granting special requests without considering stated policies can jeopardize leadership. Flexibility works best when it is decided by the group with clear understanding about how exceptions are to be handled.

If you don't have a written personnel policy, write one now! If you do have one, check it carefully for congruence with your vision. Then, review the policy with your entire team.

In defining boundaries for your employees, you remove potential fear and uncertainty for them. *Your purpose is not to control with rules and policies, it is to create a common reference for clear expectations.*

Expectations will change as your team's maturity grows. You may begin with rules and move to group agreements as individuals and team relationships matures. Enjoy the process!

Agreements

Here are some standard agreements that should to be written, discussed, and approved by each individual.

✓ **Work schedule:** Days, hours, lunches, on-time expectations, overtime, job sharing, rotating schedules, individual accountability to see that the job is done and the rest of the team is supported.

✓ **Commitments:**

- You are expected to bring ideas and solutions, with positive expectations that problems can and will be solved.
- Your attitude is very important to effective, profitable teamwork. We ask that you notice negative attitudes in yourself and do what you can to positively self-manage.
- Loyalty to your team and to your employer is defined by a willingness to express your needs and concerns to the appropriate person or group and to be accountable for your own feelings.
- Confidentiality is another expression of loyalty. We openly share statistics and numbers with each other in this practice to enhance self-directed teamwork. Please keep numbers and management information confidential.
- Confidence in each other and the doctor is critical. Your confidence in the practice and the team will be reflected by referrals of your friends and relatives, as well as the conversations you have with each other and with our patients. We encourage you to find opportunities to compli-

ment your doctor and other team members in front of and to patients. This builds confidence in yourself and others.
- We expect to provide dentistry for you and your family.

✓ **Acceptable and Unacceptable Behaviors:**

Acceptable	**Unacceptable**
· be early for work	· late, unprepared
· give compliments	· complaints without solutions
· expect the best	· negative expectations
· ask questions	· make assumptions
· talk it out	· isolate and hide out
· express concerns	· make threats
· keep commitments	· superior or inferior attitude
· offer to help	· "It's not my job..."

Note: Federal and State Laws are constantly changing. As the owner of a business the doctor is responsible to comply with the law with regard to personnel policies. Consider an employment specialist[3] or your personal legal advisor to assure compliance.

STEP 5. TRAINING

Once expectations are clear, the new employee deserves the very best training available to fit into your team. Too often in a dental practice we assume that prior experience will cover this step. Not so. We must find a way to show our new employees *what* we expect and *how* we want them to handle procedures, practices, and key issues.

---

[3]Consultant Bent Ericksen specializes in labor laws for the dental profession. Contact Ericksen, (408) 354-2869, for a proven, updated policy manual and other related materials.

Develop a competency checklist similar to the following example:

Receptionist - Business Secretary
Competency Checklist

Competence Level I

- ❏ Pleasant behavior and friendly, helpful attitude.
- ❏ Skilled telephone technique to make best first impression.
- ❏ Schedule patients.
- ❏ Confirms patient appointments daily.
- ❏ Informs patients of that day's fees.
- ❏ Capable of learning insurance billing/statements billing.

Competence Level II

- ❏ Refined communication skills to negotiate patient needs in balance with doctor and team overhead needs.
- ❏ Basic knowledge of dental procedures and scheduling rules and preferences.
- ❏ Basic knowledge of financial policy. Ability and authority to make financial arrangements with patients.
- ❏ Competence in insurance billing, tracking, and billing procedures. Familiar with aging of account process.

Competence Level III

- ❏ Solves problems.
- ❏ Offers creative suggestions and coaches others.
- ❏ Superior communication skills including sales and customer service.

Your new employee may have had training in competency level I. It is important, however, that the techniques are congruent with your practice. This is why your new team member needs a training partner to assure clear expectations and adequate orientation and training in your office.

Very often the dentist will not be the trainer. Even if the training position is a dental assistant, the dentist probably is not the expert in all aspects of the job. Therefore, the doctor can best facilitate training by coaching and coordinating efforts with the designated training partner.

❶ Get agreement from a competent team member to enter into a training partnership with the newcomer.

❷ You and your staff trainer can agree upon the specific steps and contents of training.

❸ Focus on one specific task at a time.

❹ Have the trainee practice by repeating the task daily.

❺ Monitor the learning process by observing the new employee.

❻ Use intentional listening skills to get feedback from the trainee about what they have learned and what they need more help with.

❼ Use the debrief outline on the next page for consistent (daily, weekly, or monthly) feedback.

Outside Resources

If you do not have enough team members to do the training, find someone who will work with you in that capacity. Successful former team members may be able to spare some time. Temporary services may have someone who can fill the requirements. There are many competent people who have retired from full-time dentistry, such as hygienists, business managers, and assistants who may fill the bill. Consider contacting your community college for resources or call the Academy of Dental Manage-

Training Partnership Daily Debrief

Debrief given by ________________________________

For the training of ________________________________

RE: Mastery of ________________________________

What went well today?

What aspects of this task do you feel confident about?

What are you uncertain about?

This is what I saw that went well . . .

This is what you can improve on . . .

Let me show you . . .

Show me, or tell me what you heard me say . . .

Define agreement of focus for tomorrow . . .

Time frame for mastery:

ment Consultants. It may be helpful to use audio tapes, video tapes, and staff sessions to assure adequate training. It is important to invest in getting the right person to train your team member well. The effect and benefits will be long-lasting.

When Training Isn't Taking

If the trainee has not achieved competence within the time frame established, determine appropriate action with the training partner. Do this either by resetting goals or by terminating the trainee. *Respectful honesty is a must for successful coaching and authentic leadership.*

Hiding the truth is not easily done. Nonverbal communications speak louder than words. Hiding a problem, rather than being open to addressing it, results in dysfunctional interpersonal behavior. As an authentic leader, *you are much bigger than that.* Tell the truth.

Even when you fear an angry response, be honest. Anger and unhappiness are simply expressions of feeling. Feelings are not right or wrong, good or bad. They are human nature. Clearing the air allows you to move on.

Ongoing Training

With the rapid changes in technology and in our culture, continuous training and retraining is essential. As a management consultant I sponsor monthly study clubs for professional women who work for dentists. The participants are eager to learn.

Successful people recognize the importance of continued personal and career development. Encourage your team members to participate in learning for life. When you do, both of you will be more satisfied with the jobs you're doing.

STEP 6. GOAL SETTING AND FEEDBACK

The leader and each team member should work together to create goals for their work-related development. In this case, two heads are better than one. Otherwise, done independently, a personal agenda may take precedence over organizational objectives.

Goal Setting

Goals should be stated in terms of specific and realistic results desired. State how you will measure and verify your results. (Specific goals can be quantified. If you can't associate a number with a goal, it is probably not specific enough. To that end avoid all vague, ambiguous language.) At the end of the time period, fill in the results in terms of whether goals were achieved and to what extent.

Suggest that your team member keep a copy of their goal sheet in a location where they will look at it every day. They should review their progress daily and be prepared to report on it at your weekly meeting together.

When conducting a performance feedback conference, have the employee write down their major professional goals along with the measurement standards and time frame for them. These goals should be the ones the team member feels the most passionate about – the ones worth 100-percent commitment. The goals should be compatible with the needs and objectives of the practice, as well as individual job responsibilities.

Major Goal #1

Define Strategies and Activities:

Define Measurement Standards:

Define Results:

Major Goal #2

Define Strategies and Activities:

Define Measurement Standards:

Define Results:

Major Goal #3

Define Strategies and Activities:

Define Measurement Standards:

Define Results:

Scheduled Feedback Conference

The employee feedback conference is a regular time for dentist and individual staff members to review goals and to have open communication. Use the outlines for the employee feedback conference (following) and for goal setting (previous page) to help set your agenda.

Schedule a performance feedback conference with each employee three or four times each year. Use these conversations to review goals, compare behavior to desired results, encourage, coach, direct, or delegate. The results will be an increased energy level and renewed commitment on their part.

As discussed in Chapter 5, you also may schedule feedback to support behavioral changes required to accomplish goals. These may require daily, weekly, monthly, or quarterly reports.

Your leadership style should change from being very directive at the beginning of a project, to being corrective, supportive, and finally delegating as their competence (and yours) grows.

"Leaders have a responsibility to create an environment that breeds hardiness and motivation on a ***regular****, not an occasional basis."*
–Kouzes and Posner, The Leadership Challenge

Quarterly Feedback Conference

Name ____

Attached you will find a copy of the goals we agreed upon last

_______________.

Please review our notes and comment on your perception of your own results.

I am proud to have accomplished:

____

____

I am confident that the following behaviors have become habit and no longer require goal setting focus:

____

____

Areas I would like to have your support to improve or refine are:

____

____

My goals for the next ______________ are attached.

My next feedback conference is scheduled for ____________.

STEP 7. TEAM SUPPORT

Leaders support their team in many ways. Making time for team meetings is essential. Team members feel supported when the leader pays attention to concerns and ideas that only can be expressed effectively in a participative group setting. The leader acts as facilitator at the team meetings to demonstrate commitment and focus. Then, after the team members buy into the idea, the roles of facilitator and recorder can be rotated among the group.

Effective team meetings need to have an agenda, a time frame, and successful results. If your team has an issue that you are uncomfortable in resolving, call in a competent facilitator to help you in the process. Consequently, in watching how they work, you'll be learning how to handle other such situations in the future.

If you have not developed group agreements, or have not created a mission statement, this would be an excellent place to start. Remember, it is not the final product of the written agreements or the printed mission that matters. It is the *experience of ownership* that comes from participating in the process.

Make your environment a safe place for people to be. Make it a place where people can grow. Celebrate success! Acknowledge accomplishments. Be respectful to each other. Take time to talk. Learn to be open and honest with each other. Help team members understand the symptoms of office uproar discussed in Chapter 5. Ask them to help you address those symptoms in your workplace.

Remember birthdays. Remember employment anniversaries. Create celebrations. Ask team members what they want to experience more or less of. Open the lines of communication in a non-invasive, healthy, and safe way.

Rather than striving for perfection, go for the process. Take each step one at a time and begin now.

Inspiration

Once each year take your team on a "Vision Quest." Create a ritual that breaks up the routine. Go to the beach for a retreat; go to the mountains; do a ropes course; go boating, or sailing, or skiing. Play together and make time to challenge the status quo.

Take a trusted facilitator to keep you all focused and creative. Use processes that involve the team members in clarifying their personal and career-related values. Work together to create win/win ideas and visions of how your team can be together over the next year.

Use a year calendar to plan events and celebrations. Target benchmarks and schedule individual feedback conferences.

Brainstorm ways to get feedback from your patients, your suppliers, lab technicians, accountant, and community leaders. Think about ways you can serve the community. Consider sponsoring educational events, hosting study groups, and networking through study clubs or mentor groups.

"When the staff is energized, the patients are energized. The energy feeds the fire of enthusiasm and it grows creating momentum," says one Authentic Leadership graduate. "To be creative, you've got to let go! When I released control, I found new power and huge potential."

Expand your ability to create new and relevant ideas. This is the fuel of inspiration's fire. Schedule it. Keep your schedule. Keep your word. Allow your team members to become inspired by providing an opportunity for them to stretch.

STEP 8. SALARY EVALUATION

At least once each year do a salary evaluation conference with each employee.

The purpose of this conference is to acknowledge the employee for the results and accomplishments they create. Review personnel policies and rules. Clarify expectations regarding vacation time, responsibility for temporary replacements, effect on bonus plans, and practice profit. Plan for win/win agreement. Openly discuss employees' personal goals for earnings, continuing education, and professional advancement. Ask what this person values and what motivates them.

Staff members should be paid a satisfactory salary in relationship to the kind of job they do and the results they get. Salaries should be reviewed and merit raises granted whenever they are appropriate. Many practices schedule staff evaluations twice yearly in conjunction with review of dental fees. Staff evaluations may or may not result in merit raises, but it is exceedingly important that doctor and staff members get together on a regular basis to clarify expectations and to enhance personal growth.

A letter of acknowledgment puts a pay raise in writing and defines salary and benefits in hourly,[4] monthly, and yearly terms. This letter also confirms the next salary adjustment period. It allows you to separate the salary evaluation from other performance conferences.

It is very important to state the following sentence in your letter: "You are appreciated!"

To determine what salaries should be, refer to the planning outlined in Chapter 4. Your overhead ratios provide a guideline

[4]Team members often compare their salaries with other associates based on hourly figures.

for setting goals regarding scheduling, production, and collections. By targeting total percentage of salary, you can define realistic production and collection goals for the coming year.

When goals are achieved they must be acknowledged and celebrated. Keep your word and keep your agreements.

Sample Letter of Acknowledgment

This sample is only a model. Please make all remarks in the body of your letter with care, making them germane to the specific employee and their performance.

Date:

RE: Compensation/Salary Adjustment

Dear (staff member name):

You have learned a lot in the last year. You are no longer the part-time student, but rather a responsible administrative assistant. You have shown the ability to take charge of the insurance tracking and billing system. You seem to understand your goals. You are able to get the results you desire.

(Staff member name), your knowledge of the practice and your skill in achieving specific results are appreciated.

As of (date), your hourly salary shall be designated as (new $ amt). To calculate your yearly salary, we have taken 40 hours a week x 52 weeks to equal $__________. To calculate a monthly average, we have divided by 12 to equal $__________.

Your yearly salary includes personal leave time, holidays, and vacation time as defined in our personnel policy.

Other benefits currently in effect, and paid for you are:

Medical/Dental	Life	Disability	Per Month	Per Hour
$55.01	$3.30	$18.00	$76.31	$.44

Thank you for the ideas you have shared. Your friendly rapport is a benefit to this practice! I look forward to another great year with you.

CLUE: *Written acknowledgment and thank you notes will benefit you and your employee beyond measure. I have seen women hold their letter close to their heart and cry. They take it home and proudly show it to their family. It is important to acknowledge your staff. Do it!*

BREAKDOWNS, SIDETRACKS, AND DERAILMENTS

Sometimes, although we are doing our very best, we look up and notice that we are off track. It may not be anyone's fault. It may be that something has changed and we need to blaze a new trail. It may be that the best laid plans went astray. Perhaps it was just Murphy's law. In any event, please avoid the temptation either to place blame or to take on guilt. It is important only to identify the breakdown. The more quickly the breakdown is identified, the better.

If the breakdown seems to be with a particular individual, some personal coaching may help to get them realigned. Nip problems in the bud and get back on your course.

You can always refer to the following checklist to help you through derailments.

Consider why people fail in order to help them succeed.

1. They don't know what you want them to do.
   Action: Clarify expectations.
2. They don't know how to do it.
   Action: Train them.
3. They don't know why they should do it.
   Action: Affect learning through group sharing, brainstorming, problem solving, and team planning.
4. They won't do it anyway.
   Action: Follow outline of personnel rules.
   Give written notice. Keep records.
   Terminate if there is no improvement within the specified time.

Go through the checklist to diagnose the problem.

1. In regard to this specific situation, are the expectations clear? Ask. Use your intentional listening skills. Be sure agreement of expectations is clear and set goals for corrective action.
2. Be confident that the individual has been trained adequately. If not, implement training.
3. Discuss the benefits perceived in the proposed action to be taken. Check for a mismatch in core beliefs or values.
4. When something is simply not working, you usually know it in your gut. Listen to your intuition.

In the unhappy event that you need to terminate an employee, plan ahead for it because the experience is emotionally draining. Plan to comply with labor laws and make every effort to make the parting a friendly one.

Do not keep the employee on for any period of time after termination. Be prepared to make a clean break and let the person leave immediately. This means having their final paycheck ready including any unpaid benefits. Itemize the benefits included in the check. One employee had to write her own final check. She included six weeks of vacation and a bonus which, in her anger, she felt she deserved. The doctor was so upset that he signed the check.

When terminating an employee, get straight to the point. "Sally, I'm going to have to let you go. I appreciate many of your qualities and will be happy to give you a recommendation in those areas. It may not seem like it now, but in the long run this will probably be a very good thing for you. It is apparent that *(you are not happy, or challenged, or headed in the same direction as I am)* and I am confident that you will find a place that is just right for you."

"I have your paycheck which includes (benefits and/or severance). I wish you well. Let me know how I may assist you in your search for another position."

CHAPTER 7: SELF-CHECK

- ❑ After studying the components of the leadership cycle, I will use:

- ❑ I can empower or share power with my team members by:

- ❑ Actions I will schedule yearly include:

- ❑ Next time I have to hire, I will remember:

- ❑ Checklist for new employee introduction:
  - ✓ Mission or Purpose
  - ✓ Group Agreements
  - ✓ Personnel Policies/Benefits
  - ✓ Employee Development Record
  - ✓ Training and Orientation Plan
  - ✓ Schedule of Development Feedback Conference

CONCLUSION

For continued success in today's challenging business environment, owners are required to keep the momentum of the work force directed toward growth and development. There are big changes afoot in the world, and dentistry will reflect those changes. Competition for value is already evident in the marketplace. Consumers are much more discriminating about what they buy, when they buy, and how much they pay.

They will judge the service you provide based on the performance of the whole team. Mediocre performance will not make the grade. Apathy in the work place must be transformed into positive action.

Team members will always be dependent upon the doctor to:

- be present,
- be on time,
- provide high quality care, and
- provide leadership.

In the old form of management, team members were dependent on the boss for approval. They can be "set free" from unhealthy dependence when the doctor takes responsibility as the leader to listen, talk, plan, and acknowledge them.

ACTION PLAN REVIEW

❶ Decide where you are going. Make a business plan for five years, starting with year five and working backward. As you explore these issues, your vision will come into focus.

- Where will you be?
- Who will your patients be?
- What kind of dentistry will you be doing?
- Who will your staff members be?
- What will be your reputation in the community?
- How will your peers speak of you?
- What will your financial plans require?

❷ When you have a plan and a time schedule, enroll your staff in your vision and in its benefits.
❸ Use statistical reports as planning tools. Make individual team members accountable for specific results.
❹ Schedule and hold regular coaching feedback interviews with each team member to find out what you, as their leader, can do, or stop doing, to achieve the vision you hold for your practice. Find out what each individual wants to achieve. Help them think in terms of what they want to do in five years and see if it is a match with your vision. Set goals together and schedule frequent meetings for coaching support.
❺ Create safe team meetings where creative input is shared and valued.
❻ Be authentic, direct, and respectful. Your staff members are your first line of clients. Your patients are your second line of clients, and should be cared for in the same way you care for your first line of clients.
❼ Work with a passion to develop protocol and keep it in place. Schedule follow up. Keep your word.

SOME POINTS TO REMEMBER

Free to Lead has been written to help you realize your own personal power to choose. Whether you are a dentist, an assistant, hygienist, receptionist, technician, or an industry consultant, you make a difference! Your contribution is critical.

❶ Decide what you want. Know yourself.
❷ Commit to the process of self-mastery.
❸ Be responsible. *Know that you are able to respond to any situation.*
❹ Surround yourself with "response-able" people.
❺ Tell them about your dreams.
❻ Listen to their dreams.
❼ Cooperate together to create and recreate success.

There comes a time to be absolutely, authentically who we are. It is a time to stop pretending that we are better than anyone else or fearing that we are worse. It is a contemplative time that recognizes the transforming power life brings in the experiences of both pain and pleasure. It is the time to honor the wisdom we have gathered along the way. And then, it is the time to give back a measure of the abundance we have received.

"TO WHOM MUCH IS GIVEN, MUCH IS REQUIRED"

We have been given much indeed: the opportunity to be in charge of our own destiny, to choose our own work style, our hours, our clients, and our friends.

This is the time to redefine our role – beyond fixing teeth, beyond possessing power. The leader's role is to use power by giving it away.

Paradoxically, we are set free by becoming accountable.

Like a spiral, the dynamic force of freedom grows. It gathers momentum with every person set free:

free to choose,
to go the distance,
to challenge the status quo.

The end is the beginning of the option to be Free to Lead

What do you mean "leader?"

L	Leads	Listens	Learns
E	Example	Empowers	Enables
A	Accountable	Attitude	Appreciation
D	Decisive	Defines	Declares
E	Expectations	Exceptional	Excellence
R	Responsible	Results	Return

Here is the joy to create and co-create
a new opportunity for humankind
one person at a time.

Welcome to the journey!

NOTES

BIBLIOGRAPHY AND FURTHER RESOURCES

Bandler, Richard and John Grinder. *Frogs into Princes.* Moab, Utah: Real People Press, 1979.

Bennis, Warren and Burt Nanus. *Leaders: The Strategies for Taking Charge.* New York: Harper and Row, 1985.

Bethel, Sheila Murray. *Making a Difference: 12 Qualities that Make You a Leader.* New York: Berkeley Books, 1990.

Braiker, Harriet B., Ph.D. *The Type E* Woman.* New York: Signet, 1986.

Brothers, Joyce. *How to Get Whatever You Want Out of Life.* New York: Ballantine Books, 1978.

Capra, Fritjof. *The Tao of Physics.* New York: Simon and Schuster, 1982.

----------. *The Turning Point.* New York: Bantam Books, 1984.

Castine, Jacqueline. *Recovery From Rescuing.* Deerfield Beach, Fla.: Health Communications, Inc., 1989.

Covey, Stephen R. *The Seven Habits of Highly Effective People.* New York: Simon and Schuster, 1989.

Davis, Roy Eugene. *How You Can Use The Technique of Creative Imagination.* St. Petersburg, Fla.: Great Outdoors, 1961, 1967.

Dossey, Larry, M.D. *Space, Time and Medicine.* Boulder: Shambhala Publications, Inc., 1982.

Ferguson, Marilyn. *The Aquarian Conspiracy.* Los Angeles: J.P. Tarcher, Inc., 1980.

Gordon, Thomas. *Parent Effectiveness Training.* New York: The New American Library, Inc., 1975.
----------. *Leader Effectiveness Training.* New York: Bantam Books, 1977.

Grinder, John and Richard Bandler. *The Structure of Magic.* Palo Alto: Science and Behavior Books, Inc., 1976.
----------. *Trance-formations.* Moab, Utah: Real People Press, 1981.

Hill, Napoleon. *Think and Grow Rich.* New York: Fawcett Crest, 1963.
----------. *Succeed and Grow Rich Through Persuasion.* New York: Fawcett Crest, 1970.

Houston, Jean. *The Possible Human.* Los Angeles: J.P. Tarcher, Inc., 1982.

Jampolsky, Gerald G., M.D. *Love is Letting Go of Fear.* Millbrea, Calif.: Celestial Arts, 1979.

Keirsey, David and Marilyn Bates. *Please Understand Me.* Del Mar, Calif.: Prometheus Nemesis Book Co., 1978, 1984.

Keyes, Ken.
Handbook to Higher Consciousness.
Prescriptions for Happiness.
How to Enjoy Your Life in Spite of It All.
Your Heart's Desire.
A Conscious Person's Guide to Relationships.
Taming Your Mind.
How to Make Your Life Work or Why Aren't You Happy?
The Hundredth Monkey.
Ken Keyes Center Bookroom
790 Commercial Ave.
Coos Bay, OR 97420 (503) 267-4112

Kouzes, James M. and Barry Z. Posner. *The Leadership Challenge.* San Francisco: Jossey-Bass Publishers, 1987.

Laborde, Genie Z. *Influencing with Integrity.* Palo Alto: Syntony Publishing, 1984.

Liar, Jess. *I Ain't Much, Baby But I'm All I've Got.* New York: Fawcett Crest, 1972.

Maslow, Abraham H. *Toward A Psychology of Being.* New York: D. VanNostrand Co., 1968.

----------. *The Farther Reaches of Human Nature.* New York: Viking Press.

McGregor, Douglas. *The Human Side of Enterprise.* New York: McGraw-Hill, 1960.

Melton, James, Ph.D. *Vital Enthusiasm.* Palm Springs, Calif.: Global Publications, 1983.

Naisbitt, John. *Megatrends.* New York: Warner Books, 1984.
---------- and Patricia Aburdene. *Megatrends 2000.* New York: William Morrow and Company, Inc., 1990.

Peck, M. Scott. *The Road Less Traveled.* New York: Simon and Schuster, 1986.

Peters, Thomas. *In Search of Excellence,* New York: Harper and Row, 1982.
----------. *A Passion for Excellence.* New York: Random House, 1985.
----------. *Thriving on Chaos.* New York: Harper and Row, 1988.

Phillips, Donald T. *Lincoln on Leadership.* New York: Warner Books, 1992.

Prather, Hugh. *A Book of Games.* New York: Bantam Books, 1990.
----------. *Notes to Myself.* New York: Bantam Books, 1990.

Ray, Michael and Alan Rinzler. *The New Paradigm In Business.* New York: The Putnam Publishing Group, 1993.

Renesch, John. *New Traditions in Business.* San Francisco: Berrett-Koehler Publishers, 1992.

Rogers, Carl Rd. *On Becoming a Person.* Boston: Houghton Mifflin, 1961.
----------. *Freedom to Learn.* Columbus, Ohio: C.E. Merrill, 1969.
----------. *Person to Person: The Problem of Being Human.* Lafayette, Calif.: Real People Press, 1971.

Ryan, Kathleen D. and Daniel K. Oestreich, *Driving Fear Out of the Workplace.* San Francisco: Jossey-Bass Publishers, 1991.

Satir, Virginia. *Self-Esteem.* Millbrea, Calif.: Celestial Arts, 1975.
----------. *Becoming Whole.* San Francisco: New Dimensions, 1985.
----------. *The New Peoplemaking.* Mountain View, Calif.: Science and Behavior Books, 1972, 1988.

Smotherman, Ron, M.D. *The Way to Enlightenment.* San Francisco: Context Publications, 1980.

Tanenbaum, Joe. *Male and Female Realities: Understanding the Opposite Sex.* Robert Erdmann Publishing, 1992.

Toffler, Alvin. *The Third Wave.* New York: Bantam Books, 1981.

vonOech, Roger, Ph.D. *A Whack on the Side of the Head.* New York: Warner Books, 1983.

Zigler, Zig. *See You at the Top.* Gretna, La.: Pelican Publishing, 1978.

Zunin, Leonard and Natalie Zunin. *Contact - The First Four Minutes.* Los Angeles: Nash Publishing, 1972.

ADDITIONAL RESOURCES

The *Academy of Dental Management Consultants* is a select and distinguished group of dental management consultants dedicated to high standards and leadership. The criteria for membership in ADMC requires proven expertise and the endorsement of satisfied dentists. For referrals call 1-800-451-9723 and ask for Susan.

Members of the *American Society for Training and Development* provide training to consultants, trainers, and leaders. Check your telephone directory for a local chapter.

Remember that your *local universities and community colleges* often provide evening and summer courses in human resource development. These are usually reasonably priced for noncredit hours. Watch for:

- Group Process Facilitation,
- Conflict Management,
- Assertiveness Training,
- Leadership Effectiveness, and
- Parent Effectiveness.

Consider these topics as part of your continuing education plan.

ORDER FORM

Name ______________________________ Title ______________________________

Business Name ______________________________

Phone (_____) ______________________________ Fax (_____) ______________________________

Shipping Address ______________________________

____

Mailing Address (if different) ______________________________

____

QTY AMOUNT

___ ***Free to Lead,* paperback** __________

1-3 @ $29.95 each • 3-5 @ $26.45 each • 6 or more @ $22.95 each

___ **Leaders Worksheet Kit, $9.99 each** __________

Contains all 8½ x 11 forms with permission to photocopy. Includes:

- Vision Time Future (p. 28)
- Doctor Questionnaire (p. 29)
- Adversity Process (p. 30)
- Personal Intentions (p. 32)
- Values Assessment (p. 33)
- The Mirror Test (p. 43)
- Team Survey (p. 44)
- Practice Budget Planner
- New Patient Monitor (p. 63)
- Statistical Data Monitor (p. 65)
- All Chapter Self-Checks

___ **Personal Development Journal Kit, $9.99 each** __________

Contains all 8½ x 11 forms with permission to photocopy. Includes:

- Employee Personal Development Schedule (p. 73)
- Step 1. Outline for Creating Job Descriptions and Performance Standards
- Step 4. Doctor's Clarification of Expectations (p. 128) and Team Member's Guide to Clarification of Expectations (p. 129)
- Step 5. Training Partnership Daily Debrief (p. 135)
- Step 6. Goal Setting Form (p. 138) and Quarterly Feedback Conference (p. 140)

SUB-TOTAL .... __________

SHIPPING & HANDLING (add 6%; $5 minimum) .... __________

TOTAL .... __________

Payment options (check one): ❑ Check enclosed ❑ VISA ❑ MasterCard

Credit Card # ______________________________ Exp. Date ______________

Authorized signature ______________________________

Send completed form with payment to: Derricott Dental Management, 6975 SW Sandburg, Suite 130-7, Tigard, OR 97223